"Wise men have been in short supply since at least the time of the Magi. Bob Merritt is one. He can help you make wisdom your go-to strength."

—John Ortberg, senior pastor of Menlo Park
Presbyterian Church, author of *Who Is This Man?*

"In *Get Wise*, Bob Merritt brings together profound biblical insight and decades of life experience to help us all discover God's wisdom. This book will save you years of frustration and pain if you'll begin to live its principles. Wisdom isn't about how much you know but how much you live, and I'm so thankful Bob has given us this incredible resource to help us all live in wisdom."

—Jud Wilhite, senior pastor of Central Christian Church,
author of *The God of Yes*

"Weaving personal storytelling and insight from the book of Proverbs, Bob Merritt shows us that we are not alone in our everyday decisions. God is there in even the seemingly small steps of life—and Bob reveals God's wisdom in this refreshing and practical book."

—Lee Strobel, bestselling author of *The Case for Christ*
and *The Case for Faith*

"Bob Merritt's wonderful book *Get Wise* reminds me of my dad, and that's one of the highest compliments I can give. Bob is a clear, warm guide, and the wisdom in this book is priceless. Reading *Get Wise* feels like having coffee with someone who knows more than you and wants the best for you. I loved it."

—Shauna Niequist, author of *Bread & Wine*

"Crafted with Bob's unique gift for storytelling, *Get Wise* leads you through the twelve top decisions that every person faces in life. A delightfully fun read with tons of daily application for people at all intersections of life."

—Bill Hybels, senior pastor, Willow Creek Community Church

"You make your decisions and then your decisions make you. It might not seem like it at the time, but every decision you make has the potential for enormous good or regret. *Get Wise* will show you how to make daily decisions that lead to a no-regret life."

—Wayne Cordeiro, founding pastor, New Hope Oahu

GET WISE

MAKE
GREAT
DECISIONS
EVERY
DAY

BOB MERRITT

BakerBooks

a division of Baker Publishing Group
Grand Rapids, Michigan

Published by Baker Books
a division of Baker Publishing Group
P.O. Box 6287, Grand Rapids, MI 49516-6287
www.bakerbooks.com

Printed in the United States of America

Library of Congress Cataloging-in-Publication Data
Merritt, Bob, 1957–
    Get wise: make great decisions every day / Bob Merritt.
        pages cm
    Includes bibliographical references.
    ISBN 978-0-8010-1383-6 (pbk.)
    1. Bible. Proverbs—Criticism, interpretation, etc. 2. Decision making—Biblical teaching. I. Title.
    BS1465.52.M47 2014
    223'.706—dc23   2014012780

ISBN 978-0-8010-1383-6 (pbk.)

Published in association with Rosenbaum & Associates Literary Agency, Brentwood, Tennessee.

To protect privacy, some details and names have been changed.

To Meg and Dave

Nobody on the planet
brings your mom and me more joy.

The difference between people who flourish in life and those who don't is wisdom, and they apply it to virtually every situation they face. They intuitively ask, "What's the wise thing to do?" dozens of times every day.

Contents

Contents

Acknowledgments

Thanks to Eagle Brook Church, my spiritual family in Christ—I love that your #1 passion is to reach others for Christ. I still can't believe what God has chosen to do through us. Amazing.

To our church board—your wisdom and support is unmatched. It's rare when a pastor and his board are also good friends. That means everything to me.

To the Executive Team—thanks for your devotion to the mission to which God has called us. You never waver.

To my agent, Bucky Rosenbaum—thanks for believing in me and helping me overcome my many fears.

To editors Bob Hosack and Kristin Kornoelje and all the people at Baker Books—you have made this project even more enjoyable than the first.

To Jason Strand—thanks for reading my manuscript and designing the study questions for each chapter. I love writing and teaching alongside you.

To Johanna Price, Andrea Eichen, and Amanda Lee—your edits and feedback saved the day again.

To Kris Wensmann—you see me at my best and worst and somehow remain sane.

To Scott and Stephanie Sample, Lowell and Bev Rieks, Peter and Mary Gove, and Kevin and Kathy Kirvida—thanks for opening your cabins and cliff dwellings for me to squirrel away. Your generosity is priceless.

To Mom—you pray for me every single day; there are no words.

Finally to my wife, Laurie—my deepest devotion and gratitude goes to you, my best friend for over forty-two years. These are the best days of our lives, Laur, and I can't wait to get home every day to see you. I totally lucked out, and everyone who knows us often reminds me of that. I just smile.

Introduction

Get Wise

A few months ago, my wife and I were on our way to Snap Fitness to work out, but I needed to stop at the office to pick up something that I kept forgetting.

It's always dangerous for me to stop at the office when nobody's there because it means I have to disarm the alarm; it becomes even more dangerous when I leave my glasses and phone at home.

I unlocked the front door, and the console started beeping, telling me I had thirty seconds, so I hit the code. But it didn't work. I entered the code again, and again it failed. (I later realized I was trying to enter my garage door code.)

Time's up.

The alarm started blaring, and I was in full panic mode because I had no phone and couldn't see. So I ran out to the car to use my wife's phone, but she'd left her phone at home as well. I knew within minutes we'd be confronted by the police, and I hoped to avoid that.

I *am* the senior pastor and sort of in charge, so when Laurie said, "What are we gonna do?" I said, "We gotta get out of here before the cops come!"

"You're just gonna leave?" she said in disbelief.

I jumped in the car and said, "What else can we do?"

We sped out of the parking lot with the sound of the alarm still blaring loudly behind us. Fortunately, when we arrived at the gym, one of my colleagues was there, and she had a phone in her purse, so we quickly dialed security and called off the attack dogs.

I don't know about you, but I need all the help I can get, because left to my own devices, I'm a disaster. (And that's just with easy stuff like alarms.) If I tried to navigate my marriage, a couple of kids, conflict, money, and major decisions at work all on my own without God's wisdom, I'd be a divorced, unemployed, angry little bald guy. But I'm not those things, at least not the divorced, unemployed, and angry part.

I think the difference between people who flourish in life and those who don't is wisdom, and they apply it to virtually every situation they face. They intuitively ask, "What's the wise thing to do?" dozens of times each day. I'm not saying that wise people don't make mistakes or encounter problems. The wisdom contained within the book of Proverbs doesn't isolate us from problems or guarantee a smooth and pain-free life, but it does offer God's *best* advice for the challenges we all have to face.

A proverb is a wise saying or principle that if lived out will *generally* lead to positive outcomes; if ignored, the outcomes will *generally* turn out to be negative.

And wisdom is different from knowledge or intellect. All of us know of really smart people—PhDs, CEOs, doctors, and lawyers—who lost their career, house, family, and kids because they were unwise. You can be incredibly intelligent and still forfeit the things you love the most. Don't do that.

When I was a boy, I'd read the book of Proverbs through and then start all over again. Thirty-one chapters, one for each day. Eventually, its truth became second nature to me. I love that the Proverbs are in-your-face bold. How can you beat verses such as, "Go to the ant, you sluggard" (6:6), or "Her house is a highway to the grave" (7:27), or "Wounds from a friend can be trusted" (27:6)? Writing to his sons, the author, King Solomon, holds nothing back.

Now that I'm older and my perspectives have matured, I'm seeing things in the book of Proverbs that I never saw before, and I'm able to find just what I need at just the right time embedded within its pages. I have more personal notes and key words written in the margins of Proverbs in my Bible than in any of the thousands of books I own. These words and phrases include:

A fool's end, self-control, suck-it-up wisdom, fatherly counsel, bad kids, wise feet, anger, sons and dads, lust, correction, wise heart, discipline, evil people, sexual sin, money, humility, storms, bad mouth, foolish words, great advisers, neighbors, friends, revenge, pride, quarrels, cheerfulness, deceit, motives, effort, routine, excuses, earning, saving, laziness, bad debt, failure, wealth, and don't be a jerk, sluggard, wimp, or leech.

For this book, I sifted through every verse contained in the book of Proverbs, isolated the dominant themes, and applied them to the top twelve decisions every person has to make in life—decisions about education, work, friends, fools, sex, revenge, marriage, parenting, and money. *Get Wise* takes God's wisdom and applies it to the challenges that are common to every human being.

Part 1 looks at the value of wisdom, how to acquire it, and why the wisdom of a man who had seven hundred wives and three hundred concubines can be trusted. Solomon is considered the wisest and wealthiest man in ancient history, but anyone who had that many wives is suspect at best. But I'm going to make a case for how we can glean wisdom from his pain and regret.

Part 2 is where a wise life begins and why decisions about your heart, mouth, and feet are foundational to the rest of your life. Look at a person's heart, listen to their words, and watch their steps, and you can predict what kind of life they'll have.

Life basically comes down to relationships, so part 3 focuses on the critical decisions you'll need to make about sex, fools, friends, and revenge. The wisdom in this section comes right out of Solomon's heartaches and will resonate with the deepest emotions that every human being experiences in relationships.

Part 4 brings eternal wisdom to the three most critical decisions you'll need to make about your family: how to begin well, how to build intimacy, and how to raise great kids.

Part 5 addresses the top two decisions you'll need to make about your work, the area where most of us spend forty years of our lives.

This book won't help you disarm alarms or find your glasses, but it might help you protect your heart, make great friends, save your marriage, build a great family, and succeed at work. I've spent the last three years putting my best insights and stories into print, and it's my sincere prayer that as you honor me by reading these pages, God will honor you by helping you get wise.

WISDOM, WEAKNESSES, AND GOD

1

Wisdom's Wealth

The beginning of wisdom is this: Get wisdom.
Though it cost all you have, get understanding.

Proverbs 4:7

How valuable is wisdom? If you knew that it would cost everything to get it, would you still go after it?

The Bible says that wisdom is the gateway to everything we desire in life, including longevity, riches, and honor. Proverbs 3:16 says, "Long life is in her right hand; in her left hand are riches and honor."

The Cost of Wisdom

You'll be tempted to doubt me, but I promise that every last, tortuous detail of this story is true, and it was one of the many payments I made to acquire wisdom.

When I was nineteen years old and a sophomore in college, I bought a used Kawasaki 500 motorcycle and decided to drive it from our home near Pittsburgh, Pennsylvania, to St. Paul, Minnesota, where I was going to school—a 950-mile trip. It was quite possibly the dumbest decision I had made up to that point in my young life.

And I decided to drive through the night because that's what my father used to do whenever he and Mom drove us five kids cross-country to Yellowstone or the Lake of the Woods, where he'd set up an Apache pop-up trailer in some second-rate campground with outdoor showers.

Driving through the night afforded my dad two benefits. First, he'd get a few hours of relief from us kids, who otherwise drove him insane with our relentless fighting and name-calling. Who could blame us when we were cooped up for ten straight hours in a Chevy station wagon with no air conditioning or FM radio?

The other benefit of night driving was that the midsummer heat would drop from a sweltering 98 to 92. I still remember lying beside my brother and sisters in the back of the station wagon, driving across Nebraska somewhere late at night with all four windows down, listening to the tires slap against the pavement and feeling the warm air blow across my spindly arms and legs. I thought, "This is the life." I grew up thinking that every family had a dad who drove a zillion miles across America, found a local KOA campground, and let his five charges loose to capture frogs, fish in the ponds, and shoot slingshots at pop cans.

So the only reason I chose to drive through the night is because that's what my dad used to do. It never dawned on me that I didn't have five kids tagging along with me.

To this day, I can't believe my parents let me do it. When I later asked my mom about it, she said, "We tried to talk you out of it, but you were so stubborn and determined that there was nothing we could do." I even tried to get my girlfriend, Laurie, to ride on the back with me; I thought it'd be cool and romantic. But I was delirious and stupid. We actually entertained it for a few hours until her mother caught wind of it and threatened my life.

One of the hard lessons in life is that one bad decision usually leads to another, and over the course of a lifetime, the many individual decisions we make begin to build up to form a direction that eventually determines the quality of our life. One small decision might not make that much difference, but add three or four more and those decisions build up to form irreversible directions and outcomes. Wise decisions lead to positive outcomes; poor decisions lead to bad ones.

In my case, the decision to drive a Kawasaki 950 miles through the night without sleep, or a windshield, resulted in some very painful outcomes. For starters, a Kawasaki 500 is a far cry from a Honda Gold Wing 1200, which glides along at 75 mph with barely a shimmer. The vibrations that shot through my body made my butt numb and my arms tingle before the one-hundred-mile mark. And without a windshield or face shield, I got pummeled by the wind and bugs. By mile two hundred, I felt beat up and exhausted.

The only wise move I made was to convince my friend Phil to drive his 1969 Plymouth ahead of me in case something happened. Phil was my safety valve; I was his nightmare. I strapped a sleeping bag to the back for a backrest, my dad duct-taped a three-foot-long stick on the front frame for a footrest, he said a prayer over me, I fired it up, and away we went.

Ninety miles later I ran out of gas on Interstate 80 somewhere near Youngstown, Ohio, because my gas tank held only two gallons. I hadn't thought about that. So I ran up over an embankment, found a farmhouse, and saw through the picture window a man and his wife watching *All in the Family*. (Funny the things you remember.) The man came to the door, I told him what had happened, and he said, "Sure, I've got a can out back. Just set it on the porch when you're done." Those were the good ol' days.

I grabbed the metal gas can and went running down the steep embankment way too fast. I lost control and tripped, which launched me into the air spread eagle. When I hit the ground, I landed with the gas can lodged between the ground and my throat. I've got a huge Adam's apple, and the impact smashed it. I stood up and said, "Phil, I can't feel my Adam's apple; I can't swallow."

Phil said, "Let me see." Dr. Phil looked me over and said, "Well, maybe it'll come back in a while." I thought, "Where did Phil get all his wisdom?" But it actually did come back with no permanent damage (as far as I could tell).

Eight hours later we finally reached Chicago, and I was borderline delirious. It was two in the morning. We were on the 294 toll road, and suddenly my motorcycle started to sputter. We had no tools and no mechanical skills. Phil pulled over and backed his car up along the freeway while cars sped by.

He got out of his car, walked back, and said, "What are you going to do now?"

I said, "You're going to have to tow me."

"You can't be serious," he pleaded.

I said, "Do you have any rope?"

He had an eight-foot-long piece of rope in his trunk, so we tied one end to his bumper and the other to my handlebars. He was going to tow me 450 miles from Chicago to St. Paul.

I had about four feet of clearance between my tire and Phil's bumper, so one bad move, one pothole, one quick stop, and it was over. If Phil braked too hard, I could slam into him, fly through his back window, or worse. Four feet of clearance at 65 mph gave me about half a second to react, so our timing had to be perfect.

Toll booths were also a challenge. We'd pull in, and Phil would toss in some change. He had enough time to pass through the gate, but it would come down on top of my head; one gate almost snapped off. We did that for eighty miles until we were spotted by a state trooper who immediately pulled us over. I was never so relieved to get arrested in all my life. I think God sent him as an angel of mercy, because I don't think I could've made it, even though I would've tried, possibly to my own demise. The trooper walked up to us, stared, and just shook his head. When he finally spoke, he said, "*What* are you doing?"

After he lectured us on our stupidity and how lucky we were to still be alive, I somehow convinced him to let Phil tow me a few more miles up to the Belvedere Oasis north of Chicago. Every time I pass the Belvedere Oasis I remember that horrible night when I paid a very steep price for wisdom. I parked the bike at the Oasis, crawled into the backseat of Phil's car, and fell asleep as he continued to drive. The first sliver of daylight was on the horizon.

The next day one of our roommates drove me back 450 miles to get my bike so we could haul it in his truck. I sold it to my brother the next spring for half what I paid.

The synapses in the decision-making part of a person's brain don't fully connect until the midtwenties. Teenagers are literally unable to consistently make wise decisions independent of their parents, teachers, or mentors. That's why God created parents—to help their kids make wise decisions until they're old enough to think clearly. In the meantime, parents just hope and pray their kids don't inflict irreversible damage on themselves or others.

The Value of Wisdom

How valuable is wisdom?

My *lack* of wisdom caused me to smash my Adam's apple, get arrested, lose about a thousand dollars, inflict large doses of pain on my body and psyche, and ensnare no fewer than six people in my web of misfortune. Solomon says, "People ruin their lives by their own foolishness" (Prov. 19:3 NLT).

In 1 Kings 3, a youthful Solomon is made king over Israel. God appears to him in a dream and invites Solomon to ask him for anything he wants. To God's delight, Solomon asks for "a wise and discerning heart" and the ability to "distinguish between right and wrong." God is so thrilled by Solomon's request that God makes Solomon the wisest man ever to live, and then he gives Solomon a bonus.

> The Lord was pleased that Solomon had asked for this [wisdom]. So God said to him, "Since you have asked for this and not for long life or wealth for yourself, . . . I will do what you have asked. I will give you a wise and discerning heart, so that there will never have been anyone like you, nor will there ever be. Moreover, I will give you what you have not asked for—both wealth and honor—so that in your lifetime you will have no equal among kings. And if you walk in obedience to me and keep my decrees and commands as David your father did, I will give you a long life." (1 Kings 3:10–14)

21

Part of what God seems to be saying is, "Go after wealth and you might not get anything; go after wisdom and you get wealth thrown in"—not just material wealth but "wealth" in its broadest sense of protection, health, and a full life. Go after wisdom and you get *life* thrown in.

Among the benefits that come with wisdom, God says, are riches, long life, protection, health, and a good reputation.

Riches, because people of wisdom work hard, save, eliminate debt, and don't gamble away their money.

Long life, because wise people don't ask to be towed behind a car with an eight-foot-long rope.

Protection, because wise people accumulate a reservoir of goodwill among friends who are fiercely loyal and rally to their aid during hard times.

Health, because wise people eat right, pace themselves, avoid foolish addictions, and entrust their worries to a benevolent God.

And a good reputation, because wise people earn the respect of their family and friends.

If God came to you in a dream and said he'd give you whatever you asked for, what would it be? Would it look anything like riches, long life, protection, health, and a good reputation? Then God says, "Go after wisdom." Those who pursue wisdom usually get life thrown in; those who pursue wealth often end up with little or nothing.

Dead in a Ditch

Every day after I finish writing, I go on a fifteen-mile bike ride because exercising releases those funky little endorphins that make me feel okay about the world again. After sitting with words and ideas all day, exercise also allows my thoughts to flow. Some of my best ideas come to me while I'm on my bike. Sometimes I can't get home fast enough to jot down a good idea before it floats away just as quickly as it came to me.

Yesterday I was a mile down the road when I realized I had forgotten my pack, which contains my phone, driver's license, blood type, and phone number of the cabin caretaker. I hesitated for about three seconds but then turned around to get my pack. There's not a lot of traffic where I'm staying. In fact, there's not a permanent residence within two miles. I retrieved my pack because I don't want to end up dead in a ditch somewhere. That's what John Ortberg's mom used to tell him: "You're going to end up dead in a ditch somewhere." "Not just dead," Mrs. Ortberg used to say, but "dead in a ditch."[1] What could be worse than ending your life dead in a ditch? Not much.

So I went back to get my pack. I paid a high price for that piece of wisdom thirty-five years ago—with a metal gas can that smashed my Adam's apple while I was lying face down . . . in a ditch.

There's a cost to wisdom. But it can save your life, marriage, kids, career, and whatever else you value. Solomon says, "Get wisdom. Though it cost all you have, get understanding" (Prov. 4:7). And the payoff is that you get life thrown in.

2

Wisdom for Dummies

The fear of the LORD is the beginning of knowledge,
but fools despise wisdom.

Proverbs 1:7

I don't mean to imply that anyone's a dummy, although five of
Solomon's favorite words are *fool*, *dolt*, *simpleton*, *stupid*, and
sluggard—biblical words my father occasionally used on us kids
whenever he thought we needed a little motivation. He figured
if those words are in the Bible, they must be anointed. The good
news is that wisdom is accessible to all, even the dullest among us.

Wisdom in Action

First Kings 4:29–31 says:

God gave Solomon wisdom and very great insight, and a breadth
of understanding as measureless as the sand on the seashore. Solomon's wisdom was greater than the wisdom of all the people of

the East, and greater than all the wisdom of Egypt. He was wiser than anyone else.

Shortly after God granted Solomon his request for wisdom, Solomon was presented with a problem that showcased how wise he'd really become. First Kings 3 contains a story of two women, prostitutes, who lived in the same house and had each given birth to a son. During the night, one of the women accidentally lay on her baby, killing him. The woman whose baby was still alive accused the woman whose baby had died of switching the babies during the night, giving the dead child to her while taking the live child as her own. They stood before Solomon, each insisting that the living child was her own. There were no witnesses, no husbands, no DNA verification; it was one woman's word against another's. How would Solomon decide?

Solomon said, "Bring me a sword." Then he ordered that the living child be sliced in two and that each woman get half. One woman was filled with compassion and said to the king, "Please, my lord, give her the living baby! Don't kill him!" But the other said, "Neither I nor you shall have him. Cut him in two!" (vv. 26–27). Solomon knew immediately to whom the child belonged and said, "Give the living baby to the first woman. Do not kill him; she is his mother" (v. 27). The Bible says that when all Israel heard about Solomon's verdict, the nation held him in awe because of his wisdom.

When a wise person rises to a place of leadership, everyone benefits. Solomon's wisdom blessed the nation of Israel in the following ways:

- Extensive building projects. Vast construction of the temple, palace, and fortifications employed seventy thousand laborers, eighty thousand stonecutters, and thirty-three hundred foremen.

- An impressive military force. Israel's military included thirty thousand fighting men, officers, captains, and commanders of chariots.

- Peaceful trade relations. Solomon built a massive fleet of ships on the Mediterranean Sea through which he procured goods from all over the world. Once a year, Solomon received gold from Africa that weighed twenty-five tons!
- A lucrative mining industry and a refinery on the shore of the Red Sea that allowed Solomon to export copper and iron.
- A horse and chariot trade. Solomon imported twelve thousand horses from Cilicia in Egypt. No other nation had a military machine like that of Solomon, who modernized war by adopting horses and chariots as his chief weapons.
- A monopoly on trade routes through which Solomon received a steady stream of taxes and revenue.

No wonder Jerusalem flourished. When a nation, city, school, family, or marriage is led by a wise person, everyone wins. Proverbs 24:3–4 says, "By wisdom a house is built, and through understanding it is established; through knowledge its rooms are filled with rare and beautiful treasures"—not necessarily monetary treasures but treasures of safety, goodwill, laughter, and relational harmony. Are your rooms filled with those kinds of treasures, or are they filled with broken hearts, lost dreams, and cracked photographs that are the result of unwise choices? Solomon says, "Though it cost all you have, get wisdom" because wisdom is the pathway to a full and blessed life.

So how do you get it?

Game-Changing Wisdom

In 2011, I faced a decision that required more wisdom than I had, and what scared me was that the future of our church depended on this one decision. If I got it wrong, the fallout could include financial devastation, loss of staff, and disrepute to the name and cause of Christ. If I got it wrong, we might never recover. But if I got it right, it could expand our impact tenfold. The decision was mine to make, and it was a pivotal moment in my twenty-year tenure as senior pastor of our church.

Each of us will face a handful of decisions in life that are absolute game changers: choosing what to believe about God, choosing a career path, choosing whom to marry, choosing whether or not to have kids, and choosing to stay married or to part ways. These decisions will require the best wisdom you have because they will affect your life for the rest of your life. We make our decisions, and then our decisions make us. This was one of those decisions.

We were at the halfway point of a three-year financial campaign that was funding the construction of our fourth campus. The campaign was going well, commitments were strong, and we were paying our bills. Within six months, our new campus was filled with two thousand people at four services.

But we had been dreaming and talking about putting a campus in another Twin Cities suburb for several years, and one of the determining factors was how well the fourth campus did. It was doing so well that some of us took it as a divine mandate to accelerate our plans for a fifth campus.

So we started talking about this fifth campus that on paper looked doable. We reasoned, "If we can raise this much, borrow that much, prorate it out over fifteen years, get fifteen hundred new people giving by year two, survive the pinch point at year twelve, and fill all the new staff positions with proven leaders, we're golden." I remember thinking, "That's a lot of ifs for such a monumental decision."

But architects were hired to draw up schematics, preliminary plans were laid, and talk of borrowing more money and raising several more million dollars *in the middle of a campaign* became the major topic for our leadership team and church board. As far as we knew, this had never been done in the history of Christendom, but we thought, "Where's the faith?"

But the more enthused our leadership team became, the more nervous I became. We were days away from making a monumental decision that, if it worked, would be another testament to the amazing power of God. But if it failed, it could sink us. One of the warnings Jim Collins raises in his book *How the Mighty Fall* is, "Don't blow a hole below the waterline." He says that all successful organizations take bold risks, but they avoid taking the really big risks that, if they failed, would blow a hole below the waterline and sink the whole ship.[1]

We have a great board, and their main role is to be forward thinking, so I don't fault them or anyone else for wanting to accelerate expansion. But I was so unsettled that I called an emergency executive meeting so we could go through all the details one more time. After that late-night meeting, I cornered every one of the board members, looked them in the eye, and asked them how they really felt. They each had concerns, but all said we should move forward. The same was true with my executive team. I was the only holdout.

By the way, if you think you'd like to lead a big church or business and be responsible for millions of dollars, the livelihoods of more than two hundred staff members, and the spiritual well-being of thousands of people, let me tell you it's not all that glamorous. I never signed up for this, asked for it, planned for it, or even wanted it. And I never saw it coming. Were it not for the assurance of God's calling on my life and his promise never to leave me or forsake me, I would've bailed a long time ago.

After that emergency meeting, I told my executive pastor that I still didn't have peace about it and that I needed to call another emergency meeting. I knew this upset him, because the train had already left the station and this was not the time for cold feet. Everyone was on board but me, and if we stopped now, the losses in design work, momentum, and credibility with the city council would be steep. But we spent another late night reviewing spreadsheets, fund-raising options, and income-to-debt ratios.

The very next day, I had to fly to Norway for a ten-day trip to meet with churches and to speak at the Global Leadership Summit. So I ended that meeting by challenging everyone to spend the next ten days praying about our decision. When I got back, we'd have another meeting to make the call. I left for Norway with a nagging fear that we were heading down a wrong path, but I wasn't sure. And I didn't know how I'd find the answer.

One of the voices I had rattling around in my head during this time was that of Pastor Bill Hybels, whom I remember once saying, "There will be times when all your board members and advisers will vote yes to something, but at the end of the day it's your hide. You're the one who has to raise the money, lead the charge, and ultimately assume the responsibility. There will be those rare times when you have to stand alone and say no."

I wondered if this was that time.

Whose voices do you have rattling around in your head? One of the ways you get wisdom is by putting yourself in a room with people who are better, wiser, and more experienced than you are. I do whatever I have to do—buy a plane ticket, lose sleep, shamelessly tag along to a restaurant—to get to know people who are wiser than me, because somewhere down the road I'm going to need their wisdom.

So off I went to Norway with two books stuffed in my bag: *Leading on Empty* by Wayne Cordeiro and *How the Mighty Fall* by Jim Collins. Cordeiro spoke to my spirit, while Collins spoke to my intellect, and it was the one-two punch that I needed to find clarity.

Cordeiro wrote about how he lost his passion for ministry by overloading his life with too many yeses. It wasn't the church's fault; it was Cordeiro's fault for not managing the pace of his life and for not saying no to more and more speaking, teaching, writing, and traveling. He was sidelined for six months trying to relocate his vibrant self. It was gone, smashed by a frantic pace that had depleted his serotonin levels and pushed him into depression. Serotonin is a feel-good chemical that when depleted shuts down your emotional system. Cordeiro writes, "While everyone in our great church *loves* the Cordeiro family, I have come to realize that nobody is *fighting* for my family."[2]

I sat there at thirty-five thousand feet at midnight listening to the din of the engines when I realized that I was on the front end of a major ten-day trip to Norway with a low tank. I was already on the edge, and so were many of our staff members back home. I remember thinking, "Who's holding the gun to your head, Merritt?

Who or what is driving you to risk everything and go after a fifth campus eighteen months into a major capital campaign?"

I finished reading Cordeiro and started *How the Mighty Fall.* In this book, Collins examines how once-strong, successful organizations decline and fall into extinction. Do you remember Zenith, Motorola, Rubbermaid, or Circuit City? All were once towers of success and resiliency until they fell into oblivion. And churches are not exempt. How does this happen?

Collins cites three main causes: hubris born of success, undisciplined pursuit of more, and a denial of peril. In other words, organizations become at risk when they've been successful, get prideful about it, think they can bite off more than they can chew, and then refuse to believe the danger signs. They blow a hole below the waterline but think it's not going to sink them.

I never sleep well after I fly east across multiple time zones. I toss and turn until midnight and then give up and take an Ambien. It's one of the reasons I go to Europe as little as possible. But this time I'm convinced God orchestrated the convergence of this major trip and this major issue when he knew I'd be wide awake ten nights in a row.

After I'd spend all day mentoring Norwegian pastors, I'd go to bed at 9 p.m. and lie awake until midnight staring at the ceiling and praying. My constant prayer was, "God, what do you want us to do about this fifth campus? Speak to me, show me, give me some kind of leading or sign." Every night for ten nights I lifted that prayer to God. On the last night, I sat up in bed and grabbed a yellow pad. The thoughts were coming with such clarity that I knew they were from God. On top of the page I wrote, "Twelve Reasons to Delay Our Fifth Campus." I had absolutely no doubt, no hesitation that God had spoken, and I couldn't get home fast enough.

The next day I sat across from my executive pastor and told him why I thought we should delay. He pushed back appropriately. I pushed back harder. We both knew the situation could get ugly, but we'd been around that block before and neither of us wanted to go there. So before one of us said something he'd regret, we agreed to sleep on it and meet the next day.

The next day we were still stalemated, but he yielded to my leadership. I told him, "I can't fully explain it and I don't have as much knowledge about spreadsheets, debt ratios, and interest rates as you do, but I've laid this before God and I can't get peace about it. The bottom line is that I simply can't violate what I believe is God's leading." He was disappointed, but we both have learned to listen to that voice. Now we had to inform the board, staff, and city council. The news was met with a mix of disappointment and relief.

A River of Wisdom

One year later, we opened that fifth campus but not in a new building with a mountain of debt and a burned-out staff. We opened in a high school. And they were so welcoming that they let us make improvements to their sound and lighting—*in a public school*. Being in a school allowed us to build a foundation in that community and generate the resources to build a new facility.

Before we launched in the high school, a group of board members, staff, and major donors sat in the school auditorium for a first-look tour. In that group were several businessmen, one of whom has been deeply impacted by our church. I had lunch with him a few days later, and he told me how much he hates debt and how glad he was that we pulled back on our original plan to build. He told me how important that was to him, and he complimented us on our wisdom.

Then he dropped a bombshell. He said that he wanted to chip away at our long-term debt—quietly and steadily. I asked him what he meant by "chip away." When he told me, I wasn't sure I'd heard him right, so I asked again. When he repeated it and attached some numbers to it, I was stunned. He said he wanted to eliminate $16 million of our debt in a matter of a few years. After I pulled my jaw off the table, a single thought swept over me. How valuable is wisdom, and what if we had charged ahead without it? Solomon says, "Get wisdom. Though it cost all you have, get understanding" (Prov. 4:7).

But how? I think there are four major streams through which wisdom flows.

The God Stream

Solomon's single prayer was that God would give him "a wise and discerning heart" (1 Kings 3:12). He prayed that God would give him wisdom. James 1:5 says, "If any of you lacks wisdom, you should ask God, who gives generously to all." James did not say that if we lack wisdom we should ask Oprah Winfrey, who gives generously to all, or ask our mother-in-law, or check our horoscope. He instructs us to ask God. I ask God for wisdom several times a day. Why? Because Proverbs 2:6 says that "the Lord grants wisdom."

Wisdom often has a supernatural aspect to it because sometimes it doesn't come in any other way except by asking God for it. But doing so seems so simplistic that we often don't give it much credence. Solomon says that wisdom comes from God and that we access it through "fear of the LORD" (Prov. 9:10). To fear the Lord means to have such a deep respect for God that we start every day and face every problem with an acknowledgment that he's in charge, not us. It's facing every day with a prayerful dependence on God, asking him to direct our thoughts, words, and decisions. I pray that prayer almost every morning.

So when was the last time you asked God to give you wisdom, maybe for how to deal with your son or daughter, restore your marriage, approach a conflict at work, or make a decision that requires a major outlay of money? If it's been awhile, it might be the reason you're at your wit's end. There are some decisions that will come to you only when you pray for God's wisdom and he instills it in your heart and soul. And the most difficult decisions often require an extended season of prayer. The fear of the Lord, the acknowledgment that God is in charge and you're not, is the beginning of wisdom.

The People Stream

Who are the people in your life? This is important because you will seldom rise above the quality of people who surround you.

So take a good look at your closest friends and colleagues. How wise are they, how moral, how balanced, talented, or successful? What are their marriages and families like? If you look around and all you see in your circle of friends are fools, dolts, simpletons, and sluggards, you will consistently fall short of your potential. Solomon says, "A companion of fools suffers harm" (Prov. 13:20 NIV 1984).

Who are your advisers? Whom do you go to when you're struggling with a problem and need wisdom? If nobody comes to mind, that's trouble. I handpicked six accomplished Christian men to meet with once a month so I can learn from them. Maybe there's another stay-at-home mom with whom you could exchange notes once a month. Or maybe you know someone whose marriage you admire and they're willing to mentor you.

At the same time, you don't have to know an adviser personally. I have read books by people who've made valuable wisdom deposits into my life. I read everything John Ortberg writes, as well as Bill Hybels, Henry Cloud, Andy Stanley, and John Eldredge. Solomon says, "Hold on to instruction, do not let it go; . . . for it is your life" (Prov. 4:13). When I went to Norway, I allowed two wise people to speak wisdom to me through their words. I could have played games on my iPad or numbed my brain by watching movies. Instead, I soaked in wisdom from two of the best thinkers on the planet.

The point is that you simply cannot become wise if you're not reading; you'll have wisdom gaps that will cause you to make bad decisions and block your progress. You might say, "But I don't like to read." Then get used to failure. I can't count the number of people who've come to me over the years with layers of problems who in answer to the question, "What are you reading?" have said, "Nothing." Nothing that inspires or challenges them, nothing on forgiveness, conflict resolution, or spiritual growth. And nothing from the Bible. They have a wisdom deficit that's impossible for anyone to fill. If you're a parent, for example, you're committing parental malpractice by not reading at least one good book on parenting; same with marriage, spiritual growth, or money management. The good news is that you can start closing the gap. If you read just half a chapter a day, you will get through ten books in a year.

The Experience Stream

In the last twenty-five years, I've been through six major building campaigns, all of which seemed impossible to me. They intimidated me and scared me, and in every one of them we fell short of our goal, so they also made me feel like a failure. Fund-raising campaigns and building projects are hard, and they wear me out. But with all six I gained wisdom by sheer experience.

With each of those campaigns, no matter how impossible and scary it seemed, I always had peace about moving forward. When peace was missing in the situation I described earlier, it was a signal to me. That one element, the lack of inner peace from God's Spirit, was a major factor in my final decision. But I wouldn't have been able to discern that lack of peace without the experience provided by the other five campaigns.

When I don't have enough experience, I need to get people around me who do have the experience to help me make wise decisions. There have been times when I've looked around the room and thought, "The people in this room aren't experienced enough to make this decision. We need someone at the table who's been down this road before." Sometimes you just know you don't have the right people around the table and you have to have the humility and guts to acknowledge it. If you (or your team) are too prideful and you think you know it all when you don't, you'll make costly mistakes. There's a reason why we have marriage counselors, financial planners, consultants, physicians, and lawyers. They have experience we don't have but need.

The Pain Stream

There are two pain streams through which you can gain wisdom: your own pain or by learning from someone else's pain. Pain is a powerful teacher, and it's always better to learn from someone else's pain. When you see your friend get hammered after every hockey game only to become an alcoholic who's divorced and struggles at work, you know to avoid that. Or when you see friends overspend and buy everything on credit to the point at which they can't pay their bills, you learn from their pain. You learn when you see someone who never studies in school, can't get into college, and misses out on their career dreams. Or when someone was sexually exploitive and now struggles to find a lasting relationship. Or when someone started with pull tabs and now has a gambling addiction that tanked their marriage, family, and future. It's just dumb to go through all the pain of addiction, divorce, debt, and loss yourself when you can watch other people do it, learn from their mistakes, and say to yourself, "That looks painful; I think I'll avoid that."

When a high school classmate drove off an unfinished bridge and killed himself and nearly killed another friend, I made a note to myself: Never, ever drink and drive, and never ride with someone who has been drinking. And when I learned that my grandfather was an alcoholic whose addiction impoverished his entire family, I decided at an early age that it wasn't worth drinking at all.

I am so grateful for the hundreds of people who have found freedom from their addictions in our church's recovery program, and every one of them would stand up and say to the rest of us, "Spare yourself the losses and pain of addiction. Learn from my mistakes so that you don't have to go through what I've gone through." When I see the carnage that addiction, indebtedness, sexual impurity, and divorce cause other people, I know to avoid those roads at all costs. If you've been there, the wisest thing you can do is pursue forgiveness and restoration through Christ. All of us make mistakes, which is why all of us need the loving forgiveness of Jesus.

When the four streams of God, people, experience, and pain flow into your life, they form an unstoppable river of wisdom that blesses every aspect of your life. And then Proverbs 2:10 happens: "Wisdom will enter your heart." Wisdom will become second nature to you so that no matter how dicey life gets, you'll instinctively know what to do almost every time. Life's currents will start to flow with you more than against you.

3

A Wise Man's Weakness

He [Solomon] had seven hundred wives of royal birth and
three hundred concubines, and his wives led him astray.

1 Kings 11:3

Children ages six through ten were asked a series of questions
about marriage. Their answers are delightfully honest; some even
contain a touch of wisdom.

First question: "How do you decide whom to marry?" Alan,
age ten, said, "You got to find somebody who likes the same stuff.
Like if you like sports, she should *like it* that you like sports, and
she should keep the chips and dip coming." (Pity the girl who ends
up with that kid.)

Kristen, age ten, said, "No person really decides before they
grow up who they're going to marry. God decides it all before, and
you get to find out later who you're stuck with."

When asked, "What is the right age to get married?" Freddie,
age six, said, "No age is good to get married at. You got to be a
fool to get married."

"How can a stranger tell if two people are married?" Derrick, age six, said, "You might have to guess, based on if they're yellin' at the same kids."

On dating, Lynnette, age eight, said, "Dates are for having fun, and people should use them to get to know each other. Even *boys* have something to say if you listen long enough."

"Is it better to be single or married?" Anita, age nine, said, "It's better for girls to be single, but not for boys. Boys need someone to clean up after them."

"When is it okay to kiss someone?" Pam, age seven, said, "When they're rich." (Smart girl.)

On getting married a second time, Angie, age ten, said, "Most men are brainless, so you might have to try more than one to find a live one."

And finally, when asked, "How would you make a marriage work?" Ricky, age ten, said, "Tell your wife she looks pretty even if she looks like a truck." That kid's wise beyond his years.[1]

Solomon's Weakness

Solomon could have used some of that advice. For all his wisdom, he had a gaping flaw that's almost beyond explanation. I feel compelled to address Solomon's polygamy because the Bible does. The Bible isn't a book of carefully edited prose that glosses over the flaws of its characters and heroes. It's a record of real life, sins and all.

Even the godliest people in the Bible were sinners, often embarrassingly so. Moses was a murderer and a fugitive. And then he wrote the first five books of the Bible. King David (Solomon's father) was an adulterer and a conspirator in the murder of his mistress's husband. And then he wrote most of the Psalms. Paul ordered the stoning of Stephen and made it his mission to exterminate anyone who followed Christ. And then he wrote much of the New Testament.

John Ortberg asks, "Have you ever noticed how many messed up families there are in Genesis?"

Cain is jealous of Abel and kills him. Lamech introduces polygamy to the world. Noah—the most righteous man of his generation—gets drunk and curses his own grandson. . . .

Their marriages are disasters. Abraham has sex with his wife's servant, then sends her and their son off to the wilderness at his wife's request. Isaac and Rebekah fight over which boy gets the blessing. Jacob marries two wives and takes in two concubines on the side. They get into a fertility contest.

Jacob's firstborn son, Reuben, sleeps with his father's concubine. Another son, Judah, sleeps with his daughter-in-law when she disguises herself as a prostitute. She does this because she is childless since her first two husbands—both sons of Judah—were so wicked that God killed them both. . . .

These people need a therapist. These are not the Waltons. They need Dr. Phil, Dr. Laura, Dr. Ruth, Dr. Spock, Dr. Seuss—they need somebody. (Feel any better about your family?)[2]

Ortberg then asks a key question: "Why does the writer of Genesis include all this stuff? There's a very important reason. The writer of Scripture is trying to establish a deep theological truth: *Everybody's weird*."[3] In other words, all of us are sinners in need of God's grace.

Our Weaknesses

No matter how wise we are, each of us has a weakness that if not confronted and managed can be our undoing. Solomon's weakness was women—no surprise there. This is most men's weakness. And while wisdom can often keep us from falling, it's not fail proof. All of us have a problem called depravity—all of us. The Bible says that the common denominator of every human being is sin. It's the reason we get mad, yell at each other, seethe with jealousy, hurt each other, call it quits, erect boundaries, threaten, fight, sue, and move away.

The other day my wife was mowing the grass, and I was concerned that she wouldn't finish in time to get ready for a graduation party. (She enjoys mowing, so relax.) My wife is a petite person, but when I walked up to her and shouted over the mower that she should hurry up, she shot me a look that I hadn't seen in a while but am very familiar with. And then she shouted, "I'm going as fast as I can. Back off!"

What amazed me was how quickly a fight can form. Just seconds before, my wife was happily mowing the grass on a gorgeous afternoon. I was lying on the couch watching golf, and all was well with the world. But anger, hatred, and flat-out depravity are lying just beneath the surface, and all it takes to bring them out is a little accusation.

I stood toe-to-toe with the woman I love but momentarily despised. Because we'd done that dance many times before, I knew if I shot back we'd get into it and nobody would win. Somehow I found enough restraint to do just as she said. I made a decision to put a higher value on my relationship with Laurie than on a bunch of people whose lives would go on just fine if we were late. I have failed in moments like that more often than I've succeeded, but all of us have areas of weakness that can pull us away from God and others.

Why Should We Listen to Solomon?

Solomon's glaring weakness was women—seven hundred wives and three hundred concubines. Concubines were essentially wives of lower status. If Solomon had sex with a different woman each day, it'd take him nearly three years to get to everyone. You'd have one thousand sexually starved, emotionally unbalanced wives and one completely worn-out husband. How could the wisest man ever to live have had such a glaring and self-destructive flaw, and why should any of us listen to anything he said?

Here are five reasons.

A Wise Person Is Not a Sinless Person

When left unchecked, sin will trump wisdom almost every time. Unbridled, unchecked sin is more insidious and more powerful than wisdom. In my first book, *When Life's Not Working*, I asked the question, "How can extremely wise and intelligent people do such stupid things?"[4] It's because in the heat of temptation their emotions override their intellect. People get too close to an area of temptation, their emotions kick in, and all their intelligence and wisdom go out the window. That's why I occasionally stand in front of our staff, draw a line down the center of a whiteboard, and say, "Here's the line. Don't even get near it!" Don't get near the line, because if your emotions kick in, they will override your intellect and you'll end up falling for something or someone that'll wreck your life. After losing everything, people often say, "I don't know what I was thinking." And that's the point. They *weren't* thinking. Their emotional "want to" short-circuited their intellect, and they ended up forfeiting their marriage, family, faith, or career for a temporary, emotional choice. No amount of wisdom can withstand the pull that sin has when it hooks into our emotional "want to."

So in Solomon's case, a great and wise king may at the same time be a foolish and weak king. A great and wise president may at the same time be a foolish and weak president. A great and wise CEO may at the same time be a foolish and weak CEO. A great and wise pastor, teacher, coach, husband, wife, son, or daughter may at the same time be foolish and weak. That's the power of sin. A wise person is not a sinless person.

Polygamy Became Prevalent in Ancient Times Partly Because Wars Decimated Male Populations

In ancient times, when a nation went to war, often the whole male nation went to war. Even in our American Civil War, sons fought alongside dads, cousins, and uncles. Entire families were left without even one male member.

In ancient patriarchal societies, where women outnumbered men and were considered second class at best, it was nearly impossible for an unmarried woman to provide for herself, so she relied on her father, husband, and brothers for provision and protection. Unmarried women were often subjected to slavery and prostitution.

While polygamy was not morally right, a single woman who ended up in Solomon's harem would have been protected and physically cared for.

Women Were Often Given as Gifts When Kings Signed Treaties

When kings signed treaties in ancient times, it was customary for the lesser king to give his daughter in marriage to the greater king. Every time a treaty was sealed, Solomon ended up with yet another wife as a token of honor and friendship. The ancient Babylonian and Canaanite cultures in which biblical history began were known for polytheism and polygamy—many gods, many wives. These were the two sins that God's people constantly fell into and in some respects still do today.

God Allowed Polygamy, but He Didn't Excuse It

Solomon and all of Israel suffered a great loss because of polygamy. In 1 Kings 11:11, God said that he would "tear the kingdom away" from Solomon and give it to one of his subordinates. All that Solomon had accomplished and accumulated would be lost, but not in his lifetime. Because of Solomon's father, David, God said he would withhold judgment on Solomon and pour it out on his son: "I will tear it out of the hand of your son" (1 Kings 11:12).

Sin always leads to loss. Always. Lost friendships, lost marriages, lost opportunities. God may allow sin to take place, and he may withhold his judgment for the greater good of accomplishing his work—God has always shown a willingness to use flawed men and women to accomplish his work—but there comes a point when God's patience for unrepentant sin runs out, his judgment falls, and justice prevails.

Sometimes Hindsight Is the Best Wisdom of All

A brief look into Proverbs shows that Solomon came full circle and pleaded with his own sons not to follow in his footsteps in this area. He urged them, "Rejoice in the wife of your youth. . . . May her breasts satisfy you always, may you ever be intoxicated with her love" (Prov. 5:18–19)—not wives, plural, but wife. He warned them regarding an adulterous woman, "Do not go near the door of her house, lest you lose your honor to others and your dignity to one who is cruel, lest strangers feast on your wealth. . . . At the end of your life you will groan when your flesh and body are spent" (Prov. 5:8–11). He recounted the sad ending of his own life and warned his sons, "Don't do what I did. It's fun for a while, but it has an awful, regrettable ending."

One of the reasons we can take Solomon's advice is because there's a kind of wisdom that can be acquired only through experience and pain. In Ecclesiastes 2:8, Solomon says, "I acquired male and female singers, and a harem as well—the delights of a man's heart." What did he discover? "Everything was meaningless, a chasing after the wind" (2:11). Later he concludes, "Enjoy life with your wife, whom you love, all the days . . . that God has given you" (Eccles. 9:9). It's where the joy is—one wife, one marriage, one family as God intended.

Several years ago, my brother-in-law and I invited a couple of friends to go with us on our seventeen-mile, seven-hour Boundary Waters canoe trip to a sacred place we call Hog Hole. It's a brutal trip that brings grown men to their knees, but once you're there, the fishing is amazing.

There are several spots along the way on the Horse River that look like you could just walk your canoe up or down the rapids and save yourself from unloading all your packs and hauling four tons of gear over back-breaking terrain. And there's one spot in particular that a first-timer will fall for every time. It's like what Proverbs 16:25 says: "There is a way that appears to be right, but in the end it leads to death."

When we came to this spot, we told our friends, "Don't do it. We've tried it before, and we're telling you, it has a bad ending." But no matter how much we warned them, they didn't listen. They got out of their canoe and started walking it up the shallow rapids. My brother-in-law, Oz, and I unloaded our gear and hauled everything on land.

Midway up the rapids, they started yelling, "What a disaster! The horseflies are atrocious! You hold the canoe while I try to find a way out of this." Oz and I sat on the end of the portage eating a snack, waiting in the shade. Twenty minutes later they emerged with scratches and bites all over their bodies and a big fat bruise on their egos. Oz asked, "How was the shortcut?" They never made that mistake again.

Solomon looks back on his life and says to his sons, "There is a way that looks enticing and right. But here's what I've learned about marriage, women, and temptation: Rejoice in the wife of your youth—every other path leads to regret."

PERSONAL
WISDOM

4

Wise Heart

> Above all else, guard your heart,
>   for everything you do flows from it.
>   Proverbs 4:23

One Friday night my two adult kids and their spouses were together
in our home. After we enjoyed a nice dinner, someone suggested
we rent a movie. Generally, I don't go to movies or even rent them;
the last movie I saw in a theater was *The Passion of the Christ* and
before that it was *Titanic*. I can't sit still that long, and movies are
expensive. And if you wait long enough, the movie will be shown
on television. I know, I'm old and cheap.

I'm a little behind the times when it comes to what passes as
entertainment these days. So when my twenty-four-year-old son
brought home an R-rated thriller featuring a string of bank heists,
I was unprepared.

It was rated R for violence and language, and the opening scene
had more violence and language than I'd ever seen or heard in my
life. It was shocking. I sat on our couch next to my wife while I

watched an innocent citizen get his head bashed in with the butt of an assault rifle while he lay on the floor of a bank lobby. The bone-crushing sound effects made me recoil; I momentarily looked away. Then I watched him get shot twice in the back as the camera zoomed in for a close-up of his blood pooling around his quivering body.

The range of emotions that went through me is hard to describe. Both my children and their spouses are devoted Christians who love God and truth with all their hearts. They are passionate about their faith and morals, so I wondered if they were as bothered as I was. I didn't want to shame them for watching something that I thought was totally unacceptable, and I especially didn't want to embarrass my son, who chose the movie and brought it into our home. So I sat there and hoped it would get better. Well, it got worse. I didn't think that was possible. And as I watched and listened to humanity at its worse, my spirit sank.

Your Inner Spirit

All of us have a spirit. Our spirit is the inner, living part of us that experiences things such as fear, love, anger, sadness, and happiness. It's closely connected to our thoughts and emotions and is the driving force behind all we do, where we go, and what we value.

The Bible equates our spirit with our heart, the part of us that God's Spirit wants to indwell. Ephesians 2:22 says that people who follow Christ become "a dwelling in which God lives by his Spirit." Ephesians 5:18 instructs us to "be filled with the Spirit." So as a follower of Christ, my spirit or heart is the place where God's Spirit lives. The more I allow God's Spirit to fill and control my heart, the more my heart becomes sensitive to what God wants me to do, where he wants me to go, and how he wants me to live.

The longer my spirit took in the images and language of that movie, the more wounded and sad my spirit became. I felt my spirit react within me because God's Spirit was reacting. And I knew that if I sat there any longer I would do damage to my spirit and to the Holy Spirit of God, who was speaking to me about what I was seeing and hearing. The sights and sounds were an assault to my spirit and his.

So I stood up and, without making any accusations, simply said, "I can't watch this anymore." And I went upstairs to get ready for bed. I didn't want to embarrass my kids, but I knew I couldn't allow my spirit to remain vulnerable to the damage that those images and sounds could inflict upon it. A few minutes later my wife joined me. I said, "My spirit couldn't take it." She said, "Neither could mine." I thought, "How sad if that's what we have to subject our hearts to in order to be entertained."

You might wonder why I didn't say something to my kids or forbid them to watch any further. Part of it has to do with what I know about my kids. I know that when I left the room nothing more needed to be said; that act alone spoke volumes, and I know they would use that experience to evaluate how movies could affect their own lives.

I also know that my kids are still maturing in Christ, and their spiritual sensitivity isn't the same as mine; that comes with time and growth. Had my son brought that movie into our home at age seventeen or eighteen, I would have disallowed it and tried to talk him through it. I'm sure it would have turned a little ugly, but parenting isn't a popularity contest. Even if there's a battle, kids need, and appreciate, a firm boundary.

The next morning as I was memorizing my weekend message for church, David came downstairs, sat next to me, and said, "Dad, I want you to know that I'm sorry for the movie last night. I know it offended you, and I felt really bad about it."

I thanked him for his apology. Then sensing God's Spirit nudging me, I said, "Dave, I have to tell you that I'm shocked for what passes as entertainment today."

He said, "You have no idea. That's normal. Our generation doesn't even think about or flinch at that stuff."

I said, "What concerns me is what those images and language can do to your heart. They might seep in and start to deaden God's voice in your life or cause something inside you to shift a little until eventually you form a thought pattern that turns into harmful behavior.

I know for me I have to be really careful what I expose my heart to." We chatted a little more, he apologized again, I thanked him again, I told him how much I loved him, and that was the end of it.

Your Top Priority

Solomon said to his sons, "Above all else, guard your heart, for everything you do flows from it" (Prov. 4:23).

In one sentence, he delivered three penetrating thoughts. "Above all else." Put this at the top of your list. Make this your number one priority. If you don't do anything else, make sure you do this one thing.

"Guard your heart." Protect it. Put a wall around it. Don't let anything that's harmful or impure seep into it.

"Everything you do flows from it." Your heart is the center of your life. It's the core, the source, the place from which everything else flows. Your heart is like a deep well that keeps you alive. If the well dries up or gets polluted, it can no longer sustain life. So guard it, keep it clean, protect it any way you can, because your heart is the inner spring that sustains your life.

So Goes Your Heart

In Proverbs, Solomon mentions the word *heart* forty-nine times, and he says that the heart is the source of both good and bad. A list of some of the good things that come out of the heart includes wisdom, cheerfulness, peace, happiness, discernment, and joy. Some of the bad things include lust, perversion, deceit, anxiety, bitterness, arrogance, envy, and violence.

Jesus said, "It is from within, out of a person's heart, that evil thoughts come—sexual immorality, theft, murder, adultery, greed, malice, deceit, lewdness, envy, slander, arrogance and folly" (Mark 7:21–22). In other words, our heart is what defines us. Proverbs 27:19 says, "As a face is reflected in water, so the heart reflects the real person" (NLT).

Author Dallas Willard describes it this way:

> We live from our heart. The part of us that drives and organizes our life is not the physical. . . . You have a spirit within you and it has been formed for good or bad. . . .
>
> The life we live out in our moments, hours, days, and years wells up from a hidden depth. What is in our heart matters more than anything else for who we become and what becomes of us. . . .
>
> In short, the human heart or spirit is the executive center of a human life. The heart is where decisions and choices are made for the whole person. That is its function.[1]

Willard says that as your heart goes, so goes your life. Whatever is inside your heart will determine your direction, and your direction will determine the outcomes of your life, good or bad. Your heart determines your life.

A Wise Heart

So how's your heart these days? If someone could look at your heart, what would they find? What do you value or spend most of your time thinking about? What are your inner thoughts, passions, fantasies, and fears? Proverbs 21:2 says, "The LORD examines their heart" (NLT). When God examines your heart, what does he see?

A good place to start is to look at your mouth and feet. Solomon repeatedly makes a connection between the heart and the mouth and feet—often what you say and where you go reflect the condition of your heart. For example, "A wise man's heart guides his mouth" (Prov. 16:23 NIV 1984). Or "Above all else, guard your heart. . . . Keep your mouth free of perversity. . . . Keep your foot from evil" (Prov. 4:23–24, 27). Or "If your heart is wise, then my heart will be glad indeed; . . . when your lips speak what is right" (Prov. 23:15–16).

But how do you get a wise heart? "For wisdom will enter your heart, and knowledge will be pleasant to your soul" (Prov. 2:10). How does that happen? How do you get what Willard calls "a renovation of the heart"? There are three ways.

Ask God

God is the source of all wisdom, and he gives it to those who ask. James wrote, "If any of you lacks wisdom, you should ask God . . . and it will be given to you" (James 1:5). Paul said, "In [Christ] are hidden all the treasures of wisdom" (Col. 2:3). Jesus reminds us that apart from God we can do nothing (John 15:5). Forming a wise heart is fundamentally an inside job that only God can do. A wise heart comes from him, which is why a daily prayer for wisdom is so critical to our development.

In 2008, I was all alone on the shore of Lake Superior, and I was at a point in my writing where I was going through a lot of self-doubt. I needed some help. Usually I write for two or three hours and then take a half-mile walk up a private road to let my mind sort things out. The area where I write is isolated, and during the week, nobody's around, except for a stray jogger or an occasional car.

Before my walk, I prayed, "God, speak to me by your Spirit. I need your wisdom, so if there's anything you want me to see, hear, notice, or learn, show it to me." Part of my angst during this time was that I was uncertain of the flow of my chapters and sentence structure, and what I really needed was a good editor.

I started on my walk, looked up, and saw a skinny old man about a quarter mile up the road slowly walking my way with a cane. My immediate thought was to turn around and go the other way because I wanted to hear something from God, not from some local guy who was wearing a goofy-looking Robin Hood hat, sweatpants, sandals, and black socks.

I tried to breeze by him with a quick nod and a hello, but he stopped and said, "Hello. How are you?"

So I paused and said, "Fine. Are you a local?"

"Yeah, sort of. I saw your truck parked down at that house. Can I ask what you're doing up here?"

I should have told him I was listening to the Holy Spirit of God, which might have sent him running. But I told him I was writing a book, at which point he lit up and asked me what it was about. He said he was a poet (isn't everybody) and that he lived in the little white farmhouse four hundred yards up the road. He told me that if I ever had time I should stop by. I thanked him, but I had no intention of ever stopping.

But for the next two days, I couldn't get the Robin Hood hat guy out of my mind. That evening I stood looking out at Lake Superior, and while I didn't hear a voice or see a vision, I experienced an unmistakable prompting: "Go see the old man."

I didn't want to go, and I tried to dismiss it, but this inner nudging wouldn't go away. "Was this God's Spirit?" I wondered. So I walked up the road toward his house, and I said, "God, if you want to do something here, I'm open. I'm available. Speak to me and through me."

I knocked on the wooden screen door, the old man invited me in, and it took me about two minutes to realize that God was in this.

It turned out this guy with the goofy-looking hat was a graduate of Yale and a Rhodes Scholar at Oxford University—in English literature and composition! Living four hundred yards up the road from where I was writing in Nowhereville, Wisconsin, was a brilliant scholar who taught English composition at Carlton College, was a published author, and had traveled throughout the United States, Britain, and Australia lecturing on English composition. The guy knew a thing or two about editing. For the next two hours, we talked about writing, kids, life, and God. He took my first five chapters and became God's answer to my prayer at the precise moment when I needed it.

What if I would have been closed to God's leading and wisdom in my life? What if I had ignored the prompting of his Spirit, who lives within me and wants to lead me into encounters and conversations with others? It doesn't always work that way; sometimes when I pray for God's wisdom I get an inner nudge or leaning. Sometimes God reminds me of a verse or of something someone said. Like a loving father, God delights in giving wisdom to those who simply ask him for it.

Capture Your Thoughts

Paul said, "Take captive every thought to make it obedient to Christ" (2 Cor. 10:5). One of the ways to get a wise heart is to take charge of your thoughts, because whatever you think about will inevitably seep into your heart. When you take something captive, you confine and control it so it doesn't have control over you.

What dominates your thinking? What do you think about all day long, or late at night, or when you're alone in your dorm room? Do you have control over your thoughts, or do your thoughts control you? And would you say that your thought world is obedient to Christ? Is it holy and pure, or is it constantly derailed into darkness and sin?

Whatever we watch, read, and listen to will determine what we think about, and we live in a world that makes it impossible to avoid seeing and hearing things that are destructive to the heart. All I have to do is glance at a provocative billboard on the freeway and my thoughts can go places they have no business going.

One of the ways to counter destructive thoughts is to fill your mind with images, thoughts, and experiences—worship experiences, verses, biblical teaching, inspiring books, conversations with Christian friends—that are holy and pure so that when an impure image or thought arises, you can confine it and make it obedient to Christ. I'm shocked at how quickly I begin to want something simply because I saw an image of it in an advertisement (new car, boots, golf clubs) and how those things have no pull on me when I simply don't see them.

Solomon says, "Store up my commands within you . . . and you will live" (Prov. 7:1–2). Paul writes, "Let the message of Christ dwell among you richly as you teach and admonish one another with all wisdom" (Col. 3:16). David writes, "I have hidden your word in my heart that I might not sin against you" (Ps. 119:11). David memorized and internalized God's Word so that it would make his heart wise. These writers took charge of their thoughts by filling their minds with God's truth, because the way to change your heart is to change your thoughts.

Control Your Feelings

Feelings encompass a wide range of things that are "felt." We may feel hungry, tired, warm, fearful, romantic, or happy. People talk of feeling upset, angry, or full of hate. Others feel depressed, overwhelmed, or just plain numb. "I just want to feel good," they might say.

Sometimes this comes from a heart that's been wounded by either assault or abandonment, and they want relief from their feelings of pain. This can drive them to addictions where feeling "high" becomes a relief. Pornography and acting out sexually can produce similar highs. "Addiction is a feeling phenomenon," Dallas Willard writes.[2]

If someone's heart has been severely wounded, they might even turn to destructive behaviors such as cutting to mask their emotional pain. I stood next to a fourteen-year-old girl whose heart had been assaulted her entire life. She was getting baptized that day, and as she stood to read her story in front of fifteen hundred people about how Christ had healed her heart, I could see eight or nine scars where she had cut her wrist. Her self-inflicted physical pain had temporarily relieved her from the emotional pain she was feeling.

Sometimes feelings can alert us to danger and motivate us to change something, so feelings aren't bad. They're just unreliable. If I let feelings drive my life, I would make decisions based on what *feels* good instead of what *is* good. I'd never exercise because I never *feel* like exercising. I'd also eat constantly, weigh three hundred pounds, be addicted to all kinds of things, never go to work, and overspend. I would give full vent to my anger, end relationships, self-indulge, hurt people, and live without boundaries if that's what I *felt* like doing. I'd be an overweight, divorced, impoverished, homeless, bitter, lonely man if I made decisions based on how I felt. And it would destroy my heart.

I have to control my feelings instead of allowing my feelings to control me. Paul writes, "Letting the Spirit control your mind leads to life and peace" (Rom. 8:6 NLT). Let *God's* Spirit fill *your* spirit with his wisdom, healing, and love so that you will be guided by your Spirit-filled heart and not by feelings. If you don't understand your feelings, or if your feelings are so overwhelmingly painful, seek professional help. Those feelings are telling you that something's not right.

My son was going on his first business trip. He and two other summer associates were joining six partners from his law firm on a four-day trip. He'd have his own hotel room and would be traveling with men and women twice his age. So I sent him this exact text:

> Dave—pray 4 u every morn. Have a great trip. Always remember who you are. "Above all else, guard your heart." Proverbs 4:23. I love u. dad.

Three minutes later my phone beeped. It read:

> Thanks dad. I will. I'll let you know how it goes! I'm praying for you and your writing as well. Love you too.

Four days later we stood in church together, and my eyes were wet as I heard my son worship God in full voice, praising him for his goodness and greatness. Solomon said, "Above all else, guard your heart, for everything you do flows from it" (Prov. 4:23). So ask God to fill your heart with wisdom, capture your thoughts, and control your feelings—because nothing else works in life until you do.

5

Wise Mouth

> The words of the reckless pierce like swords,
> but the tongue of the wise brings healing.
> Proverbs 12:18

The average man speaks twenty thousand words per day, the average woman thirty thousand. Which is why when a man comes home from work, all he wants to do is grunt and groan—he's out of words. But if you're a woman who stays home with two or three little kids, you're like a grenade ready to explode. You're dying for adult conversation. So you have a guy who is out of words and a woman who's going to go crazy if she doesn't talk. It's tailor-made for conflict. (These are generalities, of course. I've met men who can't shut up and women who can barely say a word.)

The Power of Words

I became aware of a couple who'd been married for many years but were struggling. In fact, the husband made it known that he'd been seeing another woman; he wanted out of his marriage. To their credit, they pursued professional help, but their systemic problems and level of dysfunction would have required years of intervention to resolve.

I don't mean to sound uncaring, but part of their problem was her verbosity—she never stopped talking, ever. She dominated conversations with our staff, volunteers, and anyone who had a pulse. And once she latched on, you couldn't get away; it was a one-way verbal fire hose.

One day I saw both of them standing in a parking lot, and I watched her spew away at him for forty-five minutes. I thought, "No man could take that." He spoke three or four sentences, but mainly he just took it. Finally, she backed him into his car and kept hammering away. After ten more minutes, he was finally able to close his door and drive off. As she started walking toward the workout facility from which I'd been watching, I knew I had to make a decision.

As soon as she saw me, she latched on. But I was ready. I'd decided to tell her the truth. I stopped her in midsentence and said, "Can I make an observation?"

To my surprise she said, "Sure."

I said, "I just watched you unload on your husband for forty-five minutes, and he couldn't say a word. What's more is that I've watched you do this with everyone you meet. When our staff members see you coming, they scatter. Nobody wants to get stuck in a conversation with you because you never stop talking."

She said, "Thank you so much for telling me that; I never knew."

And then as if she hadn't heard me, she launched into another topic. I stopped her cold and said, "There you go again. You have a huge blind spot, and everybody sees it but you. You talk way too much, and it's driving everyone away from you." Gently I said, "I know your husband has problems, and there's no excuse for what he's doing. But your talking is part of the reason you're losing him—he's had it. Again, there are a lot of issues you and he need to address, but if you don't get control of how you dominate him verbally, no amount of intervention will matter."

Proverbs 10:19 says, "Don't talk too much, for it fosters sin. Be sensible and turn off the flow" (NLT). She had never learned this truth. She loved to talk, and that's great if it goes both ways. Healthy relating requires conversation, but it also requires an equal exchange of talking and listening.

God created us as verbal beings—that we converse verbally is part of God's creative intent. But just as with food, sex, or money, if we let our words run wildly without constraint, or if they have no boundaries or are used in an abusive way, they can be deadly.

What Words Do

For a lot of people, it's not the quantity of words but the quality that matters. Even though my job requires that I speak a lot in public, when I've used up my words for the day, I'm out. So for me it's been my *choice* of words that's been a problem at times. I am pretty sure that I have done more damage to my own reputation and caused more hurt to my wife, children, and colleagues by things I've said than by what I've done. And I have missed countless opportunities to use words to encourage, compliment, and bless people. As Proverbs 12:18 says, I've used words to recklessly pierce others and have failed to use words that heal them.

Solomon says, "The tongue has the power of life and death" (Prov. 18:21). The Bible says that our words have enormous power for both good and bad, life and death, healing and hurt. A carefully chosen word can give someone hope, heal a marriage, start a friendship, or prevent a suicide. A carelessly chosen word can ruin a friendship, kill a marriage, or deaden a dream. This one little muscle in our mouth has more power than all the other muscles in our body combined, for good or bad.

Proverbs 25:15 says, "A gentle tongue can break a bone." In other words, a gentle response or a kind word has more power than brute force. Let me offer three reasons to watch your words.

Your Words Affect Your Behavior

Proverbs 10:11 says, "The mouth of the righteous is a fountain of life, but the mouth of the wicked conceals violence." Ever wonder why some people seem to get all the breaks while other people get nothing but trouble? This verse says that how we talk may have something to do with it. "The mouth of the righteous is a fountain of life." Another translation says, "The words of the godly lead to life" (NLT). The word *life* here refers to love, joy, health, prosperity, relational well-being. The quality of our words will have a direct effect on the quality of our lives.

But the opposite is also true. "The mouth of the wicked conceals violence." There's a connection between violent speech and a violent life. Violent speech tends to foster an environment of anger, fear, fighting, and loss. In other words, there's a direct correlation between our words and our behavior.

I can honestly say that as a young boy and all through my teens and twenties I did not use four-letter words. I had a strong upbringing, and I just never got into the habit of using those words. Then I met a Christian businessman who said, "Really, Bob, what's wrong with the word *hell* or *damn*? Sure, they're vulgar, they can be crude, but using them is not like taking the Lord's name in vain. Aren't they simply descriptive words that add color to life?"

I decided he was right, so I began trying it. I'd bang my shin, but instead of saying, "Darn!" I'd say, "Damn!" And I found myself saying those words a lot. In fact, it was habit forming. What scared me was that sometimes the words came out unexpectedly, like at church or around my staff, and I had a hard time controlling it. I also noticed that when I used a word like that in a conversation, it gave license for others to do the same, and the conversation would take a downward turn. I also didn't like the way those words sounded. They sounded crude and crass.

But the real downer was that my words began affecting my behavior. Whenever I used those words, I seemed to be louder, more arrogant, more obnoxious, and verbally abusive. My words affected how I treated people, and I discovered the truth of James 3:3–5: When I lost control of my tongue, I began to lose control of everything else.

So I quit. Went cold turkey. They say it takes two days to form a habit and about four weeks to stop one. So I stopped. I broke the habit before it broke me.

Your Words Can Direct Where You Go

In James 3:3–4, the writer compares the tongue to a tiny rudder on a huge ship that steers the ship even in strong winds and to a small bit in a horse's mouth that turns and controls this enormous animal. Just like a tiny rudder steers a huge ship and a four-ounce bit directs a one-thousand-pound horse, so my little tongue directs where my life goes. In other words, my tongue has enormous control and influence over my life.

Where are you headed? Where will you be five, ten, twenty years from now? What are you going to accomplish? I could give you a pretty good idea simply by listening to your conversations, to what you talk about.

If I were to ask you, "Where are you headed?" and your response was, "I don't really know," or "I have no plans," or "I'm just waiting on the Lord," that would tell me a lot about where you're headed, or not headed.

But if your response was, "I'm going to get a degree in finance and pursue a summer internship," or "I'm going to cut costs, pick up an extra job, and pay off my debt in two years," or "I'm going to volunteer at church, lead a small group, and get serious about my relationship with Christ," that would tell me you are headed somewhere.

Fourteen years ago, I sat down at my mom and dad's kitchen table in their cabin in northern Minnesota and sunk my teeth into one of my mom's famous honey rolls. My sixty-nine-year-old dad was sitting there with me, and I looked at this great man, a retired pastor of forty-some years, and I said, "Dad, how old were you when you really began to make a difference in your work and career?"

He said, "When I was forty years old. The next ten years were the best, most productive years of my life."

I looked at him and said, "I'm forty-two, and God has done amazing things in my life and in the life of our church. But I want you to know that with God's help these next ten years are going to be the best years of my life. We are just beginning at Eagle Brook, and it's going to be a fantastic run."

I'm fifty-six now, and I can honestly say that the last ten or twelve years have been fantastic. I just recently made another vow to give my very best strength and leadership in the next ten years to advance God's kingdom on earth. My prayer is that God will continue to expand our influence so that our church can impact the culture of our entire city and reach twenty thousand more people for Christ.

But what if I would have said to my dad, "You know, I think I'm just going to coast for the next ten years. I'm going to sit back, think about retirement, and not overdo it. I'm going to let God be God and see what happens." (I've given our church board full permission to fire me if I ever say or think anything like that.)

Our words have a powerful effect on where we go and what we do in life. Not only do words affect us personally, but they also infect those around us. When people hear me talking enthusiastically about what's ahead, they say, "Where do we sign up?" When you talk in bold ways and cast an exciting vision for the future, others want to jump in and help you get there.

Someone once said, "If you say you can or you say you can't, you're right." If before a soccer game you say, "We can't win," you're right. If you say, "I could never get into med school," you're right. Of course, there are some things we can't do no matter what we say, but changing our words and our attitudes can make a big difference. Words have a powerful effect on where you go and who you become.

Your Words Have the Power to Bring Life or Death

Proverbs 18:21 tells us that the tongue has the power of life and death—that what we say can actually cause someone to thrive or die. Each of us has life-or-death power in our tongue. A simple "How are you?" brings life; a simple "You make me sick" brings death. "Good morning" brings life; "What's wrong with you?" brings death. "I'm proud of you" brings life; "Why can't you do anything right?" brings death. That's not to say we can't joke and have fun; my son once called me a "ledge-headed freak." Most families and friends have a playful banter that makes life fun, but words that are playful to some might be devastating to others. Almost every day I say something I regret. I have to constantly manage my words.

Several years ago, I grabbed a cab driven by a twenty-eight-year-old New Yorker whose accent and language were right off the street. He complained about losing his hair, and I said, "Your hair's great. Look at me. I'm completely bald."

He said, "No, you're not." Then he flicked on his dome light and said, "Oh, yeah, sorry."

I said, "You just have to do what I did: marry your high school sweetheart; then it doesn't matter."

He said, "Are you still married to her?"

I said, "For thirty-one years."

With genuine enthusiasm and a little shock, he said, "That's awesome, man." Then came the dreaded question: "What do you do for a living?"

I said, "You don't want to know."

He said, "What are you, a cop?"

I said, "Worse than that."

"FBI?"

"Nope."

"Prison guard? CIA?" He was obsessed with the law, since he'd broken nearly all of it.

I said, "Seriously, you don't want to know."

"Come on, man," he pleaded. "I've met all kinds. I'll be cool."

I said, "I'm a *pastor*."

He spun around and almost drove into a guardrail, and for a minute I thought he was going to kick me out of his cab. But he said, "That's awesome, bro. Really, that's awesome." Then with a touch of remorse, he said, "Man, I'm really sorry for cursing back there. I shouldn't do that; that's kinda the way it is in New York."

I said, "Don't worry about it. That's why I don't tell people who I am. They get all weird and think they have to be someone they're not."

The cabbie said he'd met his dad only twice in his life but had tried to call him recently to "do what dads and sons are supposed to do, talk about baseball and stuff." He wanted to connect with his dad even though his dad's a junkie and left him fatherless. The cabbie has been married three years and has three kids, one with another woman, but he wants to do it right this time. He told me he drives sixty hours a week and wants a better life for his wife and kids than he had.

After he pulled up to my hotel and put his cab in park, he turned toward me and said, "Would you say a prayer for me?" So I put my hand on his shoulder, he bowed his head, and I prayed for him and his family. I prayed that he would receive wisdom and experience forgiveness. I prayed that God would heal the wound caused by his dad. When I was finished, he opened my car door, I stepped out, and he bear-hugged me. Then he said, "Thanks so much. That's awesome, man, just awesome."

I said, "God bless you, and be good to your wife."

He said, "I will. I promise I will." Then he gave me a New York handshake, pulled me in for a chest pump, and we parted ways.

Proverbs 15:23 says, "How good is a timely word." There's not a person alive who doesn't love to hear words such as, "Way to go!" "Well done!" "You look great." "Thank you." "That's awesome!" "I'm proud of you." "I'm so glad you're my son." "I'm so lucky you're my daughter." "You can make it." "I believe in you." "I'm praying for you." My heart still jumps a beat when my wife tells me that I'm a good dad or a gifted leader. I'm bald and wrinkled, but the other day someone told me that I have a good-looking face because of my strong jawline. I loved it.

Proverbs 16:24 says, "Gracious words are a honeycomb, sweet to the soul and healing to the bones." How pleasant are your words? Proverbs 12:25 says, "Anxiety weighs down the heart, but a kind word cheers it up." How kind are your words? How gentle, warm, uplifting, or encouraging are they? If you're always ready with a joke, cut, or sarcastic remark, you will poison your relationships. Try being sincere for once, and do it for four weeks straight to break the habit.

Feeling distant from your spouse? Try a kind word. Can't get along with your kids? Try giving a compliment when they do something right. Is there tension between you and a co-worker? Try giving her a note of apology or appreciation. "But they don't deserve it," you might object. Who said anything about deserving it? You have the power to bring life or death to someone in your family, workplace, or classroom right now.

Yesterday I was on the elliptical machine at the gym and I saw that one of the employees had her two-year-old son with her while she tried to clean. I said, "He's a cutie—what's his name?" Normally I don't say anything and just mind my business. What did it cost me? Nothing. But seeing how her face lit up, you would have thought I'd just given her a million bucks. I gave her a simple compliment, and it brought a little life to a young mom trying to earn a little money.

So look for everyday opportunities to make a difference in just one person's life. What's stopping you from saying one word with one of the smallest muscles in your body? One word, one muscle, one choice: life or death.

It's up to you.

6

Wise Feet

Make level paths for your feet
and take only ways that are firm.
Proverbs 4:26 NIV 1984

It sounds simplistic, but wherever your *feet* go, that's where you end up. Wherever your feet go says a lot about who you are and what you'll become. You can avoid a lot of pain and loss in life simply by having wise feet. You don't even need to be very bright; you just need feet that will keep you out of places and away from people who can harm you.

Cabin Fever

When I was sixteen years old, I was invited most Friday nights to a cabin by four of my friends. Though I played sports with these guys, I never did anything with them outside of school because their reputation for smoking pot and consuming large amounts of alcohol was legendary. They knew I did neither, and they also knew I was a preacher's kid, but because I could catch a football and shoot a basketball, they respected me.

Almost every Friday night they said, "We're going to the cabin. Come with us, Merritt, just once. You don't have to drink. Just come and hang out with us."

I never did, though I was tempted. I loved the idea of a secluded cabin somewhere in the woods where a bunch of guys could build fires and make s'mores. But I knew this cabin was trouble, and I had a hunch we wouldn't be making s'mores—rolling joints and pounding Buds maybe, but not making s'mores. I knew that going there would expose me to things that could be damaging to my life. I wanted to see the cabin in the worst kind of way, but I never did. To this day, I don't even know where it is. I do know that those four friends didn't fair well. All four were addicted before they were eighteen. One is in prison. None of them made it to college.

Often it's not intelligence or talent that causes someone to succeed or fail; it's where they go. It's not that a particular place is bad; it's what tends to happen there that's bad. My dad used to tell me, "Bob, nothing good happens in a bar." So I stayed out of bars.

Every time I drive to northern Minnesota on I-35, I pass the Black Bear Casino. It's surrounded by ten thousand lakes, great fishing, beautiful golf courses, and miles of biking and hiking trails, but whenever I pass by, the parking lot is filled with cars. I've never understood why people would spend their vacation sitting in front of a slot machine that's programmed to make them lose money. But when they have a free day or week, that's where their feet take them. They made a well-worn path to a place that depletes their money and dulls their brain.

What if their feet took them somewhere else? What if they formed a well-worn path to a dynamic church where they could worship God, make new friends, and enliven their spirit? What if they formed a well-worn path to a charity or a community service project where they could use their energy to benefit others? What if they formed a well-worn path to a fitness center to strengthen their body? Or to a new hobby or to a classroom? All it takes is a pair of wise feet that walk away from something destructive and toward something constructive.

Well-Worn Paths

What are your well-worn paths? When you look at your life, what are the well-worn paths on which your feet consistently walk? All of us have well-worn paths that make us who we are. Here's an unavoidable truth: Your paths will predict the outcomes in your life. Andy Stanley says, "Every path has a destination."[1] He adds, "And this principle is operating in your life every minute of every day. You are currently on a financial path of some kind. You are on a relational path. You are walking down a moral and ethical path. And each of these paths has a destination."[2] Take a close look at your well-worn paths, because those paths will determine the kind of life you will have.

In Proverbs, Solomon pleads with his son to walk on straight paths and avoid evil ones.

> Listen, my son, accept what I say,
>   and the years of your life will be many.
> I instruct you in the way of wisdom
>   and lead you along straight paths. . . .
> Do not set foot on the path of the wicked
>   or walk in the way of evildoers.
> Avoid it, do not travel on it;
>   turn from it and go on your way. . . .
> Pay attention to what I say;
>   turn your ear to my words, . . .
> for they are life to those who find them
>   and health to one's whole body. . . .
> Do not turn to the right or the left;
>   keep your foot from evil. (4:10–11, 14–15, 20, 22, 27)

Solomon promises his son a long and good life if he stays on a straight path. It's predictable. He says that a morally straight path will bring life and health to a person's entire being. But he says that a morally crooked path leads to death—death to marriages, relationships, careers, finances, and personal health.

When it comes to the path of sexual temptation, which is a constant theme for Solomon, he warns, "The lips of the adulterous woman drip honey, and her speech is smoother than oil; but in the end she is as bitter as gall, sharp as a double-edged sword" (Prov. 5:3–4).

Initially, she's alluring and irresistible. All it takes for most men is a little skin, tight jeans, and a look, but then she poisons them with things such as a cheating heart, accusations, a nagging personality, and threats from ex-lovers. Solomon says she's as dangerous as a double-edged sword that cuts and wounds. "Her feet go down to death; her steps lead straight to the grave. . . . Her paths wander aimlessly, but she does not know it" (Prov. 5:5–6).

People who build great lives get on constructive well-worn paths, and they stay there. They don't swerve or get pulled off by a bunch of little paths that don't seem harmful at the time but almost always turn into bigger, more destructive ones.

Road Kill

I regularly counsel people who come to me with something that's dead—dead soul, dead dream, dead marriage—because they or their spouse walked down a crooked path. I spoke with a man whose wife had an affair with their neighbor. She left him, married the neighbor, and destroyed both their families. His wife's selfish, crooked path brought death to both marriages; death to their kids, who are confused and acting out; death to both their houses, which are in foreclosure; and death to their own personal joy. This man told me that his two young boys witness their mom and new stepdad constantly fighting and cursing at each other. The relationship was alluring and irresistible at first but poison and death in the end.

As the pastor of a large church, I hear it every week: people who mismanage their money and lose their businesses or homes, dads who can't control their anger and lose their kids, spouses who get emotionally involved with another person and lose their marriages, singles who hook up and diminish their chance of finding someone honorable, businesspeople who commit fraud and lose their jobs. Weekly I encounter battles involving custody, bankruptcy, pregnant teenagers, and families blown apart by any number of bad decisions.

Have you ever walked down a path that you regret—places you wish you'd never gone, parties you wish you'd never attended, people you wish you'd never met, phone numbers you wish you'd never dialed, websites you wish you'd never visited, purchases you wish you'd never made? It happens to all of us. We've all gone down paths that led to a regrettable outcome.

But while people may spend years, even decades, trying to recover, nobody's beyond the reach of restoration. That's the message of the Bible: God sent Jesus to restore and redeem the broken. With God's help, people find healing every day, people restore broken relationships every day, people break addictive patterns every day. But it's easier to avoid the wrong path in the first place.

The Key Word Is *Eventually*

I have a friend who's a CEO at a large software company in Minneapolis. We were talking about little paths and small compromises that people make in their relationships and businesses. He said, "Any little waver, any little blemish or bad move eventually shows up. The key word is *eventually*. It might not be until five or ten years from now, but eventually it shows up. I always picture myself in a courtroom ten years from now needing to defend every choice I made before a jury."

Each of us faces hundreds of little forks in the road every day, small ones that eventually lead to bigger ones: small comments, a two-sentence tweet, a mouse click, a sarcastic response, a purchase, a simple yes or no. It might not happen right away, but eventually all these forks in the road turn into well-worn paths that result in a destination.

Some people never achieve their dreams because of a single path they took or a path someone else took. The deficits that some paths create make it impossible for the people who got on those paths to reach their dreams. Andy Stanley says, "Some dreams won't come true. Some destinations are out of reach because of mistakes we've made, and some because of mistakes others have made. Some are out of reach because of a single, bad decision."[3]

Does that mean you should give up? No. You made a mistake; don't keep making it. Don't repeat it. Proverbs 26:11 says, "As a dog returns to its vomit, so fools repeat their folly." What are the foolish things you keep repeating? Henry Cloud says, "Patterns of failure as well as patterns of success are very predictable."[4] The only thing dumber than going down a wrong path once is going down it two or three times. Don't do that.

You might have to adjust your dreams because of a mistake you made, but it doesn't mean you have to abandon them. Start going down a better path and salvage what you can in your relationships, work, and life.

How do you do it?

Start Now

The best time to get wise feet is today—not tomorrow, not a year from now but today. If you're depressed and depleted, if your life's a cauldron of ongoing pain, loss, anger, and fear, there are reasons for it. Every path has a destination. So take an honest look at your well-worn paths and get off the ones that lead to bad outcomes.

I want to say a word to the twentysomethings. Don't waste your twenties. It's a big mistake to buy into the notion that "the thirties are the new twenties," as if you can extend your aimless drift for ten more years and be better for it.

I'm in my midfifties, which shocks me. I was eighteen just three days ago. What I've come to realize is how little time you have to get educated, learn some skills, raise a family, build a career, and make money. That's a lot to do in a relatively short amount of time. And once you're forty or fifty, the direction and outcomes of your life are pretty well set. That means you need to pay attention in your twenties and thirties because the time for building for the future is short.

In her eye-opening book *The Defining Decade: Why Your Twenties Matter and How to Make the Most of Them Now*, Meg Jay writes:

> While important events take place from birth until death, those that determined the years ahead were most heavily concentrated during the twentysomething years. . . . We are led to believe the twenty-something years don't matter. . . . This causes too many men and women to squander the most transformative years of their adult lives, only to pay the price for decades to come.[5]

Jay is a clinical psychologist in private practice and a clinical professor at the University of Virginia who specializes in working with depressed and adrift twentysomethings. She points out that about 80 percent of life's most significant events take place by age thirty-five: education, skill development, career track, marriage, determining where to live, home purchase, and starting a family. "As thirtysomethings and beyond we largely either continue with, or correct for, the moves we made during our twentysomething years," she writes.[6]

She counsels countless twentysomethings who are approaching their thirties but who are unmarketable for both love and work—who never got started and "wind up with blank resumes and out-of-touch lives."[7] She says they lack what's called "identity capital"—real-life experience, internships, a track record, something that distinguishes an individual and gives him or her a marketable identity.

Jay describes how aggravated she gets while sitting in front of a directionless twentysomething who floats into her office holding a six-dollar latte, flops down in the leather-back chair, kicks off her Toms, hikes up her jeans, and constantly interrupts their session by fielding incoming chirps on her phone. Jay says:

> I have seen countless twentysomethings spend too many years without perspective. What is worse are the tears shed by thirtysomethings and fortysomethings because they are now paying a steep price—professionally, romantically, economically, reproductively—for a lack of vision in their twenties.[8]

Jay's message is simple: Don't waste your life. Get going. Get on the education path, work path, skill development path, healthy relationships path, and volunteer and internship path. Get off the aimless bar-hopping, hooking-up, and waiting-for-your-real-life-to-start path. I love what Solomon says about a bad path: "Avoid it, do not travel on it" (Prov. 4:15). Even a five-year-old can understand that.

Both my kids were working by age twelve gaining skills, making contacts, dealing with people, and getting a leg up on every kid who sat at home playing video games and drinking smoothies. At age twenty-six, my daughter, Meg, had her master's degree in child psychology, a job in the public schools, and a marriage to a med student. At age twenty-five, my son, Dave, had his law degree, a law firm job in Minneapolis, and a marriage to a twenty-four-year-old engineer. All four went to college, played sports, worked as many jobs as they could, volunteered, got internships, and stayed sexually pure and spiritually grounded during their teens and twenties. Now they're set up to build a great life in their thirties, forties, and beyond.

If you're on a bad path, get off it and get on a better one. Start today.

Wasted some of your twenties? It's the same advice: start today. It's never too late to get on a better path. No matter how far behind you are, you can still carve out a good life with healthy relationships and meaningful work. It'll be harder and take longer, but I know dozens of people who got a counseling degree at age forty-five and fulfilled a dream; or lost their first marriage, learned from it, and have a great second one; or failed to influence their kids spiritually but are dialed into their grandkids. I talked to a thirtysomething recently who said:

> I wasted large parts of my twenties; I may have even forfeited the ability to have biological children. But God can still redeem, heal, and even use the pain and failure to accomplish other things. I probably wouldn't have my children or be married to my husband had my twenties been different. I wouldn't have *this* life, and I can't imagine that.

The longer you wait, the harder it gets, but it's never too late to get on a better path.

Stop Swerving

Proverbs 4:27 says, "Do not swerve to the right or the left; keep your foot from evil" (NIV 1984).

Sometimes you're not on a bad path, but the way you're walking it is bad. Therapist Marcus Bachmann told me, "I can't tell you how many times I've heard people say, 'I think I married the wrong person,' so they start swerving. Usually they didn't marry the wrong person. What's bad is how they conduct themselves *in* their marriage."

So often it's not that you married the wrong person or chose the wrong job. It's that you're going about it in the wrong way. You might be on the right path but have the wrong attitudes, wrong behaviors, wrong friends, wrong influences.

Recently, I spoke to our church from Revelation 2, where God warns the church in Thyatira to stop tolerating "that woman Jezebel, who . . . misleads my servants into sexual immorality" (v. 20). The church in Thyatira was tolerating, even approving of, sexual immorality, and God threatened the most severe judgment on them if they continued.

I used that passage to tell our church that we will always be a church that adheres to biblical ethics of sexuality, that teaches that sex is reserved for marriage between a man and a woman, and that sexual purity and abstinence is the standard for everyone else. I said that churches that approve of those who live together outside of marriage, have sex outside of marriage, or engage in same-sex marriage will, according to Revelation 2:20, suffer God's judgment.

Immediately following that message, a couple came up to me and said, "Well, we're living in sin." They were both divorced with kids, and they had moved in together to help the woman financially because, as a single mom with three kids, it was hard for her to make it. I get that. Most single moms are forced to carry an unfair load. There is nothing easy or fair about being a single mom or dad. But the reality is that this couple decided to swerve and walk down a path that has a bad ending. He continued to rationalize their decision, and when he was done, he said, "But we're open to hearing your advice."

I said, "Well, I applaud your honesty, and I can't begin to imagine how difficult and lonely your lives are right now, but you're on a path that promises nothing but regret and loss. For starters, every study shows that those who live together have a higher rate of abuse, a higher rate of infidelity, and a higher rate of divorce if they eventually do get married. When kids are involved, studies prove that they have a higher rate of substance abuse, more trouble in school, and a higher rate of emotional disorders. Kids are the biggest losers when their parents live together outside of marriage—no matter what age they are, it confuses them and sets them up for a lifetime of relational failure."

I softened my voice. "This is a path that has innumerable downsides and zero upsides, and God won't honor it. He can't. I can't quantify it for you or tell you exactly how it happens, but I've never seen God bless those who live together. Instead, he seems to remove his protective blessing from those who openly disobey him in this area."

"Maybe we'll just get married then," he said.

"Don't do *that*!" I pleaded.

"You both need at least six months of professional counseling separately to work through why you were divorced in the first place and what kind of residual scars you carry because of it. Then once you deal with your own junk, you need about six more months of intervention as a couple to see if you can live with each other's junk."

I continued, "And blended families are extremely complex. Raising your own kids is hard; raising someone else's kids is beyond hard. It can be done but not without extensive intervention and high levels of emotional and spiritual maturity in both of you." They stood staring at me, quiet. I give them credit for taking the punches.

But I wanted to say even more. I've seen so much wreckage from couples who live together that I felt like grabbing them and saying, "Avoid it! Run. Don't even think about it! That path has a predictable destination, and it's not good." Family therapist Bill Harley writes, "The most dangerous relationship for women is co-habitation . . . and boyfriends of single moms commit one half of all child abuse."[9]

I told them that most people in their shoes have options they haven't even thought of. He or she could:

- temporarily move in with a parent, sibling, or friend
- help the other financially without moving in together
- live on less
- look for cheaper housing
- ask for help with the kids
- cut excess costs such as cable, internet, and eating out
- trust God to honor their obedience

I said, "Why don't you do the right thing and then trust God to honor it? Why don't you move out, get counseling, and get on the right path?" Too many people cut themselves off from God's miraculous intervention. Who knows what God might do if they just obey him. God loves to meet us at the cliffs of uncertainty. They didn't give me an answer, but I'm hopeful.

Henry Cloud says, "People stop bad patterns every day; they turn their unfair lives around every day; they move out of bad relationships every day; they overcome addictions every day; they get on better paths every day."[10]

It's not intelligence; it's wise feet.

The Power of a Good Rut

Generally, ruts are negative things. You don't want to be in a rut for too long because you can get stuck. People will say, "I'm in a rut at work," or "My dating life's in a rut," meaning they're stuck. Here's the thing about ruts: they're formed by well-worn paths that have been traveled over and over. The longer you're in one, the harder it is to get out.

Some of you are in a ten-year rut; some are in a twenty- or thirty-year rut. Some of you've accepted your rut and given up. That's why it's important to get on the right path early, because when you travel the same path over and over, it turns into a rut, and ruts are hard to get out of.

But just as a bad rut is hard to get out of, so is a good rut. I'm in a thirty-four-year rut with my wife. You know who loves our rut? Our kids. They've reaped a lifetime of love, joy, security, and memories because of it. Their success is a direct result of the path Laurie and I have been on together for thirty-four years.

Our grandkids will love our rut. My family and friends love our rut and derive great confidence and hope from it. Our church loves our rut; they're banking on the promise that Laurie and I will be on the same path and in the same rut for the rest of our lives.

The pictures on our wall tell the story of a deeply entrenched, well-worn path. We've had our share of potholes, ice storms, and high winds, but our rut is cut so deep from traveling the same path together that nothing short of death will pull us out of it.

So how are your feet?

Wise feet on the right paths are key to making great decisions every day.

RELATIONAL
WISDOM

7

Wise Sex

With persuasive words she led him astray;
    she seduced him with her smooth talk.
All at once he followed her
    like an ox going to the slaughter.

Proverbs 7:21–22

Dangerous Curves

I'm no Brad Pitt, but when I was a junior in high school, I at least had hair, was the captain of our basketball team, wore bell-bottom pants and frilly shirts, and really liked girls. In fact, I thought about girls every day—more than anything else. And I wondered if they thought about me. A mere smile or look from an attractive girl could pull my focus off basketball or math for a week. I loved how girls looked and smelled; I loved how they wore their hair and colored their eyes. There was nothing that captured my attention more in high school than girls. It's all we guys talked about.

And then it happened. I was sitting in study hall in our high school auditorium when one of the prettiest, most well-endowed girls in our class walked up behind me, dropped a note in my lap, and then kept walking toward the front in her form-fitting top and smokin' hot jeans. I opened the note, and it said, "You and me, anytime, anyplace, just let me know." She signed her first name with a smile underneath it.

Based on her reputation, I knew exactly what she meant; pretty steamy stuff for a seventeen-year-old kid with raging hormones. This was a no-strings-attached invitation to a ride on the wild side that I would never forget; she'd make sure of that.

To this day, thirty-nine years later, I can still see that note and remember the rush of emotion that surged through my body. For the next few weeks, she did everything she could to lure me into an encounter that would be sensually overpowering but spiritually damaging. Intellectually, I knew that this temporary thrill would bring long-term regret. But would that knowledge be enough to resist her?

I knew that whatever I did with her offer would affect the rest of my life for good or for bad. Even at the age of seventeen, I knew what the Bible said about caving in to sexual sin and the consequences that came with it. I knew if I accepted her invitation it would damage my relationship with God, scar my soul, embarrass my family, ruin my reputation, and terminate any long-term relationship I might have with Laurie Thompson, whom I had begun to date. While my hormones were screaming yes to this note, my brain was saying, "Don't be stupid. Don't throw your future away for a temporary thrill."

It's sad, because that kind of brazen behavior in a girl usually comes from a deficit, a void she's trying to fill, a rejection of some sort—a parent who was absent or uncaring, an abuse, or even her parents' divorce, which left her empty and craving love. The ability to resist came from an abundance of care, instruction, and love from my parents. We don't get to choose whether we start from an abundance or a deficit. We only get to choose which path we will walk.

As for Laurie Thompson, she was the girl of my dreams, the girl every boy at Neshanock High School wanted to date. She was drop-dead gorgeous with soft green eyes, a killer smile, intelligence, and wholesomeness—way out of my league. After three months of telling me no when I asked her for a date, she finally agreed, reluctantly, to go with me on a double date to our class play. After that it was more rejection, followed by lame excuses and flat-out avoidance, but I persisted. I even drove up to her family's cabin three hours away in upstate New York and dropped in on her unannounced. It was a bold move. When I suddenly appeared on their dock, where she was sunbathing, she was horrified. She quickly grabbed a towel, covered herself, and said, "What are *you* doing here, and how did you find me?"

But somehow I was able to win her over, and we dated for the next three years. After high school, we went to different colleges and were separated by one thousand miles and four more years, but we stayed committed to each other through countless letters and phone calls. We were very much in love.

Worth the Wait

For seven years, through high school and college, we stayed loyal to each other and pure for each other. We spent lazy summer evenings in our small Pennsylvania town holding hands, taking walks, and sitting close. Many of those evenings faded well into the night way past my curfew, and I'd have to speed home on my Suzuki 185. I can still feel the cool night air hit my face, and with the smell of Laurie's perfume still on my shirt and her kiss still fresh on my lips, I never felt more alive. There's nothing like young love.

We kissed each other a lot those summer nights and steamed up the car windows a few times, but we knew where the line was, so we honored her strict Catholic upbringing and my puritanical Baptist morality. After seven years of dating and waiting, we wondered what our wedding night would be like.

As a Baptist preacher's kid, the thought of seeing a naked woman was scandalous to me, practically illegal; I could barely hold it inside my head. The only premarital counseling we had was a one-hour session with my dad, who at the end of it tossed us a book on sex and said, "Here, read this before you, you know . . ." We both howled in laughter when Laurie read parts of it to me on our way to our honeymoon.

After our wedding, we packed up my 1969 Mercury Cougar and took off for a two-week honeymoon to Maine, New Hampshire, and Vermont, but our first stop was the Pocono Mountains in northeastern Pennsylvania. The Poconos are a known honeymoon spot nestled in the Allegheny Mountains with canopy beds and heart-shaped Jacuzzis; we'd read about it in *Bride Magazine*. We opened the door to our honeymoon suite, saw the heart-shaped Jacuzzi, dropped our bags on the floor, and said, "Let's go to dinner."

We were nervous but excited, so after dinner we walked around for a while. When we finally stepped inside our suite, Laurie put her arms around me and whispered, "Meet you in the Jacuzzi in five minutes." It was almost more than my Baptist heart could handle. That was thirty-four years ago, and I'm still the luckiest man on earth married to the most beautiful woman on earth.

Think about it. Thirty-four years of waking up together, eating together, sleeping together, being intimate with each other, laughing together, having kids together, crying together, watching television together, building our family and life together. But here's the thing. All of that would be gone, *all* of it, had I said yes to the note. I would have forfeited it all had I agreed to a half-hour, self-indulged thrill.

In this chapter, I want to make a case for wise sex, and I have my work cut out for me, because usually we hear just the opposite. We hear about stupid sex—sex before marriage, outside of marriage, and during marriage with other partners. On television a happily married couple who doesn't cheat, swing, divorce, or become involved with a neighbor or co-worker is an oddity of the highest kind. Many college students no longer date; they go to bars and then hook up like its normal behavior. It's fun for a while perhaps, but it's also deadly.

Wise Sex

Solomon holds nothing back when it comes to the benefits of sexual purity and the devastation associated with sexual impurity. Solomon has lived the regret, shame, and relational carnage that his own sexual impurity has brought to himself and his family. He comes full circle and says that if he had to do it all over again he would have been faithful to "the wife of [his] youth" (Prov. 5:18). He equates sexual impurity to fire in his lap (Prov. 6:27), an ox going to the slaughter (Prov. 7:22), and "a bird darting into a snare, little knowing it will cost him his life" (Prov. 7:23).

Look what he says about wise sex:

> Drink water from your own well—share your love only with your wife. Why spill the water of your springs in the streets, having sex with just anyone? You should reserve it for yourselves. Never share it with strangers. Let your wife be a fountain of blessing for you. Rejoice in the wife of your youth. . . . Let her breasts satisfy you always. May you always be captivated by her love. (Prov. 5:15–20 NLT)

See the words *rejoice*, *satisfy*, and *captivated*? Within the context of marriage, God wants our sexual expression to be joyful, satisfying, and focused exclusively on our spouse. Sometimes people wonder if Christians are against sexual expression. Not at all. The Bible encourages full sexual expression within the context of marriage between a man and a woman. It was God who created sex and gave us the desire for sexual expression.

Betsy Ricucci says, "Within the context of marriage, no amount of passion is excessive. Scripture says our sexual intimacy should be exhilarating."[1] And Gary Thomas writes:

> God made flesh (humans), and when God made flesh, he created some amazing sensations. While the male sex organ has multiple functions, the female clitoris has just one—sexual pleasure. By design, God created a bodily organ that has no other purpose than to provide women with sexual ecstasy.[2]

Part of God's plan is for human beings to enjoy sexual pleasure. But what does God say about wise sex?

Wise Sex Waits for Marriage

Right now some of you are rolling your eyes and groaning in protest, saying, "Bob, you're crazy. Nobody does that, nobody saves sex for marriage. Open your eyes. You're out of touch and irrelevant."

Before you tune me out, let me pose a question: If you're a guy, who would you rather marry, a woman who's been sexually intimate with a dozen or more other men or a woman who's been sexually pure and waiting to give herself fully to the man she marries?

And if you're a woman, would you rather marry a guy who's been sexually active all through his teens and twenties or a guy who's sexually pure and respects God and women enough to wait?

Young people often ask, "So how far can we go?" My response is, "How far would you like your future spouse to go with the people they're presently dating?" The response is, "Not very far." Even my son's law school friends who drank like sailors and hooked up on the weekends confessed to him, "We go to the bars and nightclubs just to have fun. Of course, we'd never *marry* someone who's a part of that scene; we all want what you and Sara have." These young men were happy to hook up with various young women but immediately dismissed these women as marriage material. Note to young women: wise up! Even the most depraved guy doesn't want a long-term relationship with a girl who's been around.

The Bible says that the biggest reason people should wait until marriage to have sex is because sex is not just physical. The sexual experience is so spiritually intimate that when a man and woman come together sexually they become one—united in body *and* soul.

When two people have sex, they become one physically and spiritually, which is why people who are sexually active before marriage have a hard time achieving relational oneness and sexual intimacy *after* marriage. Every time they have sex with someone different, it's not just a physical union; it's a deeply spiritual union that unites their souls. And when that union is broken, there's a tearing of the soul that never fully heals. If people do that two, three, or twenty times, their souls become so calloused that the ability to experience intimacy and oneness in a marriage is virtually lost. I once stuck my tongue on a frozen lake in below-zero weather—it ripped my skin off and left me bleeding. That's what happens to people's souls when they unite sexually and then tear themselves apart.

So promiscuous people not only carry around a torn-up soul but also limit their marriage options and struggle to achieve intimacy if or when they eventually do marry. You can't have a history of hooking up and expect to have a regret-free future. The emotional damage, physical comparisons, jealousies over past lovers, and bitterness over past hurts that people dump into their marriages are very difficult to overcome.

Can someone be forgiven and restored through new life in Christ? Yes. Forgiveness and restoration through faith in Christ is the central message of the Bible and is accessible to all. But while forgiveness is free, the consequences associated with one's past often linger for years.

Is it unrealistic to expect young people to wait for marriage to have sex? If I hear one more expert say, "Kids can't control themselves today, so let's give them condoms and birth control and teach them how to have safe sex," I'm gonna puke! How dare they think so poorly of our nation's young people?

A CDC study found that the percentage of high school students who have remained virgins has risen from 45.9 percent in 1991 to 52.2 percent in 2007.[3] These are the wisest and happiest students who are setting themselves up for a great future. The percentages drop (29 for females and 26 for males) in the nineteen to twenty-four age group, but even in that category the numbers are trending up.

Don't tell me young people can't control themselves. I did, my wife did, my two kids and their spouses did. Laurie's two sisters and their husbands did, all of their children have, and their marriages and families are better because of it. There's nothing like going to bed with your spouse of thirty-four years knowing that there's never been somebody else and you belong to each other 100 percent. Let's hold young people to a higher standard, and they just might reach it. Proverbs 5:15–18 says, "Share your love *only* with your wife. Why spill the water of your springs in the streets, having sex with just anyone? You should reserve it for each other. . . . Let your wife be a fountain of blessing for you" (NLT). The Bible says that wise sex waits for marriage.

To those of you who haven't reserved sex for marriage, God offers you forgiveness and a second chance. Start your sexual purity today and let God begin to restore you. Your scarred past will make it harder for you to achieve your goals, but people get help every day, people overcome loss and shame every day, and people meet new people every day. With God's help and wiser decisions, you can carve out a better future.

Wise Sex Is Exclusive

Solomon says, "May you rejoice in the wife of your youth. . . . May her breasts satisfy you always, may you ever be captivated by her love. Why be captivated, my son, by an adulteress?" (Prov. 5:18–20 NIV 1984). The message here is one of exclusion—one man, one woman, one marriage, focusing exclusively on one another's body as the soul source of sexual pleasure.

The word *captivated* means to focus intensely on, be enraptured by, or be infatuated with to the exclusion of everyone else—hard to do when images of bronze-skinned beauties are a mouse click away. But that's why exclusion is so critical to keeping sexual expression vibrant with the one to whom you're married or will be married.

Let's be honest. After a few years of marriage, sex can become passionless and routine because it's with the same person, over and over again, and nothing is new and exciting. Toss in a few extra pounds, exhaustion, and aging, and it can be tough. This is where many people lose it. The shine wears off, so they open the door to something exciting and new. Then when *that* wears off, they go looking again, and again, only to find that the shine always wears off.

Contrary to what some people think, having multiple partners, looking at porn, and divorcing one person for another are not the ways to increase sexual intensity and pleasure. It's like the first time I saw the towering redwood trees in California. When I saw my first redwood, I almost put the car in the ditch. Two hours later, after I'd seen hundreds of them, the thrill was gone. Exposure doesn't intensify desire; it dulls and dilutes it. The more you spread your sexuality around, the less intense and intimate it becomes, and then you're just hooking up with a body.

Solomon says, "May her breasts satisfy you *always*." The Bible wouldn't say that if it wasn't possible. Anytime a man lets his focus wander toward other women, whether real or imagined, the intensity for his wife is diminished and he becomes less satisfied with her sexuality. But when he shuts off all other images and thoughts of other women and focuses exclusively on his wife, and she on him, their sexuality becomes more intense and intimate.

As a married person, your spouse is your only option sexually. So you have to find ways to keep sex fresh, alive, and invigorating. It's possible to do, even at fifty-six, and the most powerful asset you have is exclusion.

The Problem with Pornography

In the United States, pornography is a $12-billion-a-year industry. One half of all search-engine requests are for pornography. The problem with pornography is that it hijacks your sexual desire for your spouse, or your future spouse, and places it on someone or something else that frankly doesn't exist. These perfect bodies are pure fantasy. Have you been to the mall or beach lately? Perfect people don't exist in real life.

Porn heightens sexual intensity for something you can't have, which in turn generates a craving for release. But as with any addiction, as you progress in frequency and exposure, it takes more to stimulate the intensity. Eventually, there are not enough raw, deviant poses and pictures to satisfy the level of craving you've created.

Finally, you find that although you're addicted, pornography has actually diluted your ability to get excited sexually. You've been exposed to so much that nothing is intense enough to satisfy you. At that point, you're not even functioning like a human being but more like a sex-crazed animal. Any chance for a healthy, God-honoring relationship is greatly diminished.

The Choice Is Yours

There are four critical choices you must make to keep yourself sexually healthy and vibrant.

Decide Who You Want to Be

Define your relational goals, what kind of person you want to be, and what kind of marriage and family you want. Then practice the behaviors *now* that will get you there. I knew early on that I wanted to marry someone who was sexually pure and spiritually grounded. That meant *I* had to be sexually pure and spiritually grounded. That decision has to be made long before you're in a make-out session and your passion has dismantled your brain.

White-Knuckle It

If you have destructive sexual habits, you need to stop. I have a friend who told me that when he was confronted with his use of porn by a Christian mentor, he had to "white-knuckle it" for a while. The first week of abstinence was brutal; the second week was less so. He hasn't looked at porn for nine years, and now he's free.

Cultivate Other Interests

Sex is great, as God intended. But what are you going to do for the remaining 23.5 hours each day? If sex is all you think about and live for, you'll have a frustrating and pathetic existence. Try having a relationship. Get creative at work, travel, garden, cook, bike, work out, or read a great book.

Get Around Relationally Healthy People

Relationally healthy people exist, but you won't find them in nightclubs and bars. Your friends have enormous influence on your behavior, so take a look around—are your friends morally sound and spiritually passionate? Or are they morally base and spiritually dead? It's tough to be sexually wise when your friends are sexually stupid.

Best Gift of All

My son had been married for two weeks when I asked him, "Are you glad you waited until marriage?"

He gave a nervous chuckle and said, "I'm so glad. Sara and I waited for three years, and everything you and mom said about sexual purity is true. It's such an amazing gift that we brought to each other. But you know what's an even better gift, Dad?"

"What?"

"The obedience piece. We were obedient to God, and that makes us really glad. We have friends who got engaged, and because they figured they were committed, they went ahead and started having sex. I'm so glad we didn't do that. We believe part of the reason God is blessing us in so many ways is because we honored and obeyed him in this area."

If you're in the dating stage, don't forfeit that future conversation you might have with your son or daughter someday. Don't cheapen what God has called holy and sacred and reserved for marriage. Don't rob yourself and your future mate of the blessings that God has in store for those who obey him. If you've already crossed that line, start on the path of sexual purity today so that with God's help you can redeem some of what you've lost and open yourself to a better future.

The best and most frequent sex is happening between married couples who saved themselves sexually and are completely and hopelessly captivated by each other. I've been away for three days writing this chapter, and it's time for me to go home, say hi to the dog, and kiss the one I've loved for thirty-four years. Who knows what might happen after that.

8

Wise Fools

Better to meet a bear robbed of her cubs
than a fool bent on folly.

Proverbs 17:12

I was leading a meeting, and there were seven of us sitting around a table. I'd been sitting a lot that day, and after two more hours of sitting in this meeting, I was tired of it. Sometimes I just stand up and stretch a little, but this time I decided to turn around and kneel on my swivel chair, which is something a child (or a fool) might do, but I was among colleagues and friends, and it worked fine as long as I kept the back of the chair leaning against the table.

But then I thought, "Why not do a little spin one time around?" So I shoved off, and it took about half a second to realize this was a bad idea. Centrifugal force immediately took over, and I fell face forward over the backside of my chair and crashed to the floor. On the way down I yelled, "Whoa!" This was followed by a loud, clamoring bang of hard plastic and metal slamming against the floor. I went down. Hard. People in other rooms wondered if something had hit the building or fallen from the ceiling.

At first there were audible gasps, then silence, followed by uncontrollable laughter. People howled, cried, and snorted while I lay there in a pile. Pastor Jason Strand was the only one who showed any sort of compassion. The last thing he had seen from across the table was my rear end pointing skyward and the bottom of my shoes. Then I had disappeared from his sight, so he stood up and asked, "Are you all right?" Our executive director of weekend services was beet red, our executive producer held her hand over her mouth, and Campus Pastor Jason Anderson had a facial expression that said, "And this is our leader?"

Flat on my back, I looked up at Campus Pastor Don Graffam, who was sitting closest to me, and asked him why he didn't try to save me. Through laughter and tears, Don said, "I was so embarrassed I had to look away." Way to be there for me, Don.

I rolled over, got up off my hands and knees, and with no help from Don, put my chair up and sat down. But then we started laughing until we cried, so we called it a day and ended the meeting early.

Have you ever knelt backward on your swivel chair in a meeting and fallen over in front of all your colleagues? I consider myself to be a fairly wise person, but I've got a little bit of fool in me. Sometimes I'm a wise fool. During such displays of utter foolishness, my wife will often remark, "If people only knew."

Well, now you know.

A Fool by Nature

But there's a difference between being foolish and being a fool. Everyone trips up and does foolish things at times, but some people are fools by their very nature. A fool is a fool *all the time*.

I like Jeff Foxworthy because his comedy is usually wholesome, and he likes to hunt. In his stand-up routines, he sometimes talks about rednecks. He says, "You just might be a redneck if . . ." and then he gives character traits that make one a redneck.

Now there's nothing wrong with being a redneck. But just like certain identifiable traits make one a redneck, certain identifiable traits make one a fool. Solomon says, "You can identify fools just by the way they walk down the street" (Eccles. 10:3 NLT). Fools have identifiable traits—it's who they are.

Sadly, some of you have a parent who's a fool, or a brother or a sister. When you're together as a family or in a social setting, that person's foolishness can dominate the room. You may have a foolish boss, friend, child, roommate, or colleague. You might be married to a fool.

How do you know if someone is a fool? Here's a quick test. Whenever you're around this person, if you typically feel manipulated, taken advantage of, exasperated, wronged, abused, shamed, or hurt by their behavior and comments, you're most likely dealing with a fool. Normal people might make you feel like that once in a while, but they ask for forgiveness. Fools make you feel like that all the time, and they never ask for forgiveness.

Look at this verse: "Pound on a fool all you like—you can't pound out foolishness" (Prov. 27:22 Message). There's a kind of hopelessness when you're dealing with a fool, because no matter how hard you try, nothing ever changes.

Wise, Foolish, Evil

In the books *Bold Love* and *Necessary Endings*, Dan Allender, Tremper Longman, and Henry Cloud make distinctions between those who are wise, those who are foolish, and those who are just plain evil. (These distinctions are important because you can't relate to a wise person the same way you relate to a fool or an evil person.) Allender says that the difference between a fool and an evil person is one of degree. "In many respects, an evil person is simply a more severe fool who has progressed to a level of foolishness that is deeply severed from human emotion or goodness."[1]

Cloud adds, "Evil people are not reasonable. They seek to destroy. They actually want to hurt you."[2] Cloud notes that fools will often hurt you as well, but the difference is that evil people *want* to hurt you; their actions are intentional and more severe. When dealing with fools, you need to establish firm boundaries and enforce consequences; with evil people, you often need police protection and restraining orders. Evil people are generally more obvious. It's when dealing with fools that life gets more complicated.

So what are the traits of a fool, and how should we deal with them?

The Traits of a Fool

Fools Are Always Angry at Something

Proverbs 29:11 says, "Fools give full vent to their rage." Proverbs 12:16 says, "Fools show their annoyance at once, but the prudent overlook an insult."

Do you know someone who's mad at something or someone most of the time? Fools are angry at something or someone every day. They are mad at the government, their parents, their boss, their job, their spouse, their neighbors, their siblings—you name it. They're just mad.

It was a bluebird morning on the south shore. Purple lupines lined the road, and a cool breeze was coming off Lake Superior. I stopped to talk to a guy who was sitting in his flower garden pulling weeds. I said, "Good morning. How are you?"

"I don't know. Thinking about moving to Canada."

"Canada? Why Canada?"

"This country's screwed up."

I said, "How so?"

I shouldn't have asked, because from there he went off on how the government's screwing the people, how the unions have bailed on their promises, and how the whole country has gone to hell.

He was surrounded by beauty, but he wasn't seeing it. Proverbs says, "Fools show their annoyance at once" (12:16). It doesn't take long for anger to surface in a fool. This man was bitter, all alone, and divorced. He has three kids and a couple grandkids who never come to see him, so he's thinking of moving to Canada, where he can be bitter and alone all over again. The problem is that no matter where he goes, that's where he'll be—still full of anger, full of bitterness, and all alone. What a sad life. Fools are angry, and it's usually someone else's fault.

Everyone gets angry, and some anger is good when it's directed at things like injustice, child abuse, and human trafficking. But everyday anger is a poison. And it's a danger to all your relationships. A fool is almost always angry or on the verge of it.

Fools Have a Toxic Tongue

Proverbs 20:3 says, "Every fool is quick to quarrel." Fools have a snap response to every comment whether it's invited or not, and it's typically sarcastic and hurtful. "The mouth of the fool gushes folly" (Prov. 15:2).

I struggle sometimes with verbal misconduct, but a fool has a toxic mouth all the time. I have a sharp tongue that can cut and hurt people. I hate this about myself. I've done damage to myself and others by things I've said or how I've said them. I carry a lot of regret and shame over that. Sometimes I wish I had a filter built into my mouth that would catch all the stupid, hurtful things before they spill out. Some of my behavior comes from arrogance—thinking too highly of myself. That's one of the dangers with an increase in influence and visibility. It's easy to start thinking things like, "I'm important," "I know more," "I've earned the right," or "People should listen to me." But I think it mainly comes from being self-centered; I just want my way. It's sinful and ugly.

Fools also love slander. "Whoever . . . spreads slander is a fool" (Prov. 10:18). (I fail at this more than I should, but I'm trying to overcome it.) Fools are slanderous all the time. Whenever I need to talk to someone about another person who is not in the room, I try to talk about them as if they *were* in the room. If I wouldn't say something if that person were present, then I probably shouldn't say it, because it could be slanderous. Slander erodes trust and credibility with my colleagues. If I'm willing to talk poorly about someone who's not present, that makes others nervous about what I might say about them when they're not present. Fools don't care about this. Talking poorly of others is a fool's way of making themselves feel superior to others.

Look at the warnings Solomon gives to those who are verbally toxic:

> The mouth of a fool invites ruin. (Prov. 10:14)

> A fool's proud talk becomes a rod that beats him. (Prov. 14:3 NLT)

> The lips of fools bring them strife,
>   and their mouths invite a beating. (Prov. 18:6)

> The mouths of fools are their undoing,
>   and their lips are a snare to their very lives. (Prov. 18:7)

Solomon warns that a fool's mouth will ruin, beat, undo, and ensnare him. Some people don't know why they ruin friendships, can't move ahead at work, and feel constantly beaten down. Sometimes it's their foolish, hurtful, slanderous mouth that won't shut up. Most fools have big mouths that do a lot of damage, but ultimately they end up hurting themselves.

Fools Never Apologize

Fools won't apologize, because they're too weak to admit they're wrong. Proverbs 12:15 says, "The way of fools seems right to them." They have blinders on, and since they're not open to feedback or correction, they won't be able to see or admit their error.

You will never hear a fool say, "I'm sorry," "I was wrong," or "Will you forgive me?" They don't have the strength of character or relational awareness that allows them to admit error. If there's a problem or a conflict, it's always someone else's fault, and therefore it's the responsibility of the other person to apologize or fix it. If you never apologize to your spouse, children, or friends, that's a problem. It reveals a lack of character strength.

Laurie and I were at a restaurant, and a young waitress came up to our table and said, "Can I start you off with a $3 beer or a $5 margarita?" Everyone knows this is a sales technique, so without thinking, I said, "How about a free water?" I wasn't nice about it, and as soon as it came out of my mouth, I thought, "What a jerk." Our waitress walked away with her head down, clearly dinged by my insensitive comment.

For the next five minutes, God's Spirit just beat on me, convicting me of what I'd done. So as soon as our server returned with our drinks, I said, "I am *so* sorry for being snotty a minute ago; please forgive me."

Her name was Toni. Toni lit up and said, "No problem; don't worry about it." Then she cocked her head a little, pointed at me, and said, "You're the pastor at *that* church."

I thought, *Oh crap.* "Yes, I'm the pastor at *that* church."

She said, "Well, a couple of my friends over there said to me, 'Do you know who's sitting in your serving area? That's our pastor.'" Toni's friends were so excited that she had this *amazing* privilege of serving us, and I almost blew it with one stupid comment. It turns out that Toni's friends had invited her to our church many times, and she was warming up to it. We chatted a little about God and faith, and at the end, we were able to invite her as well.

Thankfully, I was able to recognize my sin and apologize for it. Think of the fallout had I not done that. I might have offended Toni, probably confirming her perception that Christians are rude and cheap. I might have pushed her further away from a relationship with Christ. I might have embarrassed her friends, who had been gently leading Toni along in matters of faith. And I might have damaged the reputation of our church and churches in general and tarnished our witness in the world.

But I asked her to forgive me. Fools don't do that; fools don't apologize. Their pride and weakness of character won't let them.

Fools Hate Knowledge and Truth

Proverbs 18:2 says, "Fools find no pleasure in understanding." They live in denial of the truth, because if they accepted the truth about who they are, it would be too painful for them. If they accepted the truth that they are angry, toxic, hurtful, petty, simpleminded, manipulative, sarcastic, and unlikable, they'd be crushed and deeply wounded. They'd have to confront the deficits in their past that cause them to lash out in foolish ways, and that would be too painful and exhausting. It's far easier to deny the truth, excuse their behavior, and rally support from those who are equally foolish.

With truth and knowledge come responsibility. Now that I know my flaws, what am I going to do about them? Will I deny them, or will I own them and try to change them? It's much easier to deny the truth and keep living like a fool.

A fool is not someone who never gets angry; we all get angry. A fool is not someone who never spouts off; we all say stupid things. A fool is one who gets angry and says hurtful things but refuses to accept the truth, own it, and do something about it.

Truth and knowledge confront my normal way of behaving; truth and knowledge force me to look at things in a new way and then adjust my behavior. Doing so takes humility and work, two things fools don't have and don't want to do. Proverbs 1:7 says, "Fools despise wisdom." This is why it's hard to talk to fools—they're not open to truth or correction. In fact, they often react with anger and violence.

Fools Repeat Their Patterns

Proverbs 26:11 says, "As a dog returns to its vomit, so fools repeat their folly." Fools repeat the same hurtful behaviors; they follow predictable patterns. A problem can usually be solved; a pattern is a behavior that is repeated over and over and is resistant to change.

Fools don't get angry and say toxic things some of the time; they do it all of the time.

If your mother has always been manipulative, buying your affection with gifts only to treat you like dirt if you don't repay her with favors, what makes you think she'll be different next week? If your father has always been verbally abusive, what makes you think his behavior will change next month? If your husband has always come home drunk on Friday night, what makes you think it won't happen next Friday night?

By the way, patterns don't change by having a conversation and hoping the pattern goes away. It takes more than a conversation to get someone to change their pattern of anger, abuse, addiction, or dishonesty. Cloud writes, "If you've had this conversation sixty-three times, do you really think that number sixty-four is going to do the trick?"[3] Proverbs 23:9 says, "Do not speak to fools, for they will scorn your prudent words." Talking to fools about their destructive patterns won't cut it. So what does it take to get a fool to change?

How to Handle a Fool

You will encounter fools all through life, and you need to learn how to deal with them. You need a set of "fool skills," because fools don't play fair and they can hurt you.

Get Clarity on the Problem

If you have a parent who's a fool, you might not even realize that she's a fool without some professional guidance, because her dysfunction is all you know. You might have a *sense* that she's a fool, but you're not clear on the behaviors that make her a fool. All you know is that you feel lousy, manipulated, or taken advantage of every time you're around her. Before you try to solve the problem, you have to know what it is.

It took a full year in front of a professional counselor for me to see that I had a problem with anger and harsh words. You'd think a guy like me could figure that out on my own, but that's how blinding patterns can be. I knew something was wrong because my wife and church board kept telling me. I just didn't know what it was. Now I know and I have hope. Get clarity on the problem.

Expose the Fool

Since talking to a fool about their pattern doesn't work, you have to expose them, usually with the help of professional guidance. Sometimes this requires a well-written letter in which you lovingly but matter-of-factly point out the destructive patterns, how those patterns have affected you, and why you will no longer put up with them. And you must be prepared. A confrontation with a fool will require planning, thought, energy, and timing. This type of strong and loving interaction will not be warmly received, so you also have to be prepared for the fallout.

When a fool has been exposed, they usually react with anger, threats, abusive language, and wild accusations. Fools react this way in order to cope with deeply hidden feelings of failure and loss. Many fools have experienced profound emotional, physical, or even sexual abuse themselves; many were abandoned by a parent or loved one, which is why they lack the inner strength to relate in a healthy way. Their only hope is professional help and spiritual healing that comes through knowing Christ.

When you expose a fool, they will feel betrayed by you, and there's no predicting how things will turn out. It could be the beginning of the end for your relationship, and you have to be emotionally and logistically prepared for that. You have no control over their response, nor can you force a fool to change their pattern. What you do have control over is how much you're willing to be around them and be hurt by them.

Set Limits and Consequences

Cloud says, "With fools, talking usually does nothing, and only consequences matter.... The only time they get it is when it begins to cost them something."⁴ Allender writes, "A fool will not repent unless he feels pain."⁵

You have to communicate things such as:

Until you get treatment and get sober, I won't be living with you anymore.

Your anger and yelling are hurtful to me, so the next time it happens I will leave.

Until you can treat my spouse with respect, we won't be coming over anymore.

Because you're perpetually late, I'm giving the account to someone else.

When you're relating to fools, you have to set limits and deliver consequences so they'll feel the pain of their bad behavior.

Several years ago, we had a musician show up ten minutes late to every rehearsal. He wasn't a fool, but his behavior was foolish. Week after week, he walked into the auditorium, fiddled with things on stage, and then joined the rest of the twenty-five people who were on time and waiting for him. It vexed me. I instructed our lead guy to talk to him about it, which he did, several times. I personally asked him to be on time. I got a smile and a nod.

I really like this person, and he's one of our best musicians. We need him. But the message I was sending to the team was that if you're a star you can violate our values and get away with it, that if you're really talented you can show up late, make the rest of us wait, and compromise our service. I decided that our values of excellence and professionalism were more important than any one person, even a highly talented one. I was done with being frustrated, losing credibility, and compromising our service.

So the following weekend when he arrived late, I gently took him aside in private and said, "What's it going to take to get you to show up on time?" I reminded him that he was a leader and that I expected better than that from our leaders. But I'd been down that road before, and I knew that talking wouldn't do it; it needed to cost him something to get him to change. So I said, "What's it going to take, five dollars a minute?"

His eyes got big. "Probably," was his response.

The next weekend he was five minutes late. I calmly went over to our producer and said, "Dock his pay twenty-five dollars this week."

Somewhat shocked, she replied, "Really?"

"Really! That's five dollars a minute."

The following week he was right on time.

He had to decide if being late was worth losing pay, and the decision was no longer mine but his to make. Cloud calls this "self-selection." You put the ball in the fool's court and let them "select" the outcome. I finally set a consequence that had some sting to it, and he responded. The only way to get a fool to change their behavior is by using cost and pain.

The world is full of fools, and the numbers seem to be growing. You and I increasingly need to be able to identify a fool's harmful traits and learn how to deal with them. If you live, work, or go to school with a fool, nobody wins by tolerating their destructive patterns. Our Christian faith requires us to make an effort to appropriately confront and correct a fool, but nobody can force a fool to change. Even Jesus said, "Do not throw your pearls to pigs" (Matt. 7:6). Some people are like swine who take pearls of wisdom and correction and trample them in the mud. It takes discernment to know if someone is even capable of receiving correction.

If you've been seeing yourself in these pages and have stayed with me, good for you. That means there's hope. A hardened fool would have tossed this book a long time ago. If you want to move from foolishness to wisdom and improve your relationships, get better jobs, and become a happier person, you need the following:

Awareness—you have to know what your foolish pattern is.

Humility—you have to cultivate a soft spirit that's open to correction and change.

Professional advice—nobody can overcome foolishness by themselves.

True spiritual growth—through regular Bible reading, prayer, and worship. Let God change you by his Spirit.

Confession—confess to those who have been most affected and hurt by your foolishness.

I consider myself to be a fairly wise person, but I still fall off my chair at times. I can be a wise fool, which is why awareness, humility, advice, spiritual growth, and confession will be a regular part of my life—and maybe yours as well.

9

Wise Friends

> A friend loves at all times,
> and a brother is born for a time of adversity.
> Proverbs 17:17

When I was in the middle of eighth grade, our family moved from Illinois to Pennsylvania. It was hard. The first day I survived my morning classes because classes were structured with little interaction between students, but nothing could prepare me for the terror I faced at lunchtime. I was escorted to the cafeteria by another student who'd been assigned to the "new kid," but when we arrived, he promptly abandoned me and joined his friends at their table.

I stood in the doorway of that noisy cafeteria holding the bag lunch my mom had packed for me, and I knew that while, legally, I could sit anywhere, socially, I couldn't. I stood paralyzed in fear, and I honestly didn't know if I had the fortitude to survive that moment without some kind of emotional breakdown. I felt sick to my stomach; the lump in my throat was triggering moisture in my eyes. I don't remember ever feeling that lost or alone.

The need for belonging is overpowering. I longed for a person, any person, to notice me and signal that it'd be okay for me to sit at their table. C. S. Lewis wrote an essay on this subject called "The Inner Ring":

> In every society, in every school, church, and workplace there are little groups of people who are on the inside. No one actually votes on who gets in, but whether you're a member or not will be reflected in subtle things—use of nicknames, inside jokes, invitations to certain events.[1]

Then he adds, "One of the most dominant human elements is the desire to be inside the Inner Ring and the terror of being left outside."[2] In order to write words like that, Lewis must have experienced the terror of being left outside himself.

I stood there terrified of being left outside when suddenly out of this noisy mass of kids emerged two eighth-grade boys. Their names were Kevin and John; they were my lifeline. My need for friendship was so deep that it felt like they were angels sent from God. Kevin was noticeably short, and John had a receding hairline that was accentuated by his greasy, long hair.

I wouldn't have chosen them as friends—at Hufford Junior High, where I'd come from in Illinois, I enjoyed inner-ring status as the captain of the basketball team. There I hung with the "in" crowd, but the "in" crowd was nowhere to be found that day—just a couple of outer-ring kids who had room at their table for a new friend.

As I look back on my life, one of my biggest regrets centers around a choice I made about eight months later. I was now well into my ninth-grade year. Kevin and John had stayed loyal and true from day one, but basketball season had arrived, and within a few weeks, I had moved very quickly from outer-ring to inner-ring status. For eight months, Kevin and John had been my only true friends, but one day we were eating lunch together when I looked up and there stood Dan. He'd been sent as a messenger from the jock table. "I've been sent to ask you to join our table," Dan announced.

This was an invitation to the inner ring, an invitation to move from the outside to the inside, from being a nobody to being somebody.

I wish I could tell you I passed the test and stayed true to Kevin and John. But I didn't. I didn't have the character to resist the inner-ring invitation. I was weak. I so craved inclusion that I picked up my lunch and followed Dan to the other table. That was the last time Kevin or John ever spoke to me.

For more than forty years, I've been ashamed of my decision, and I've regretted it. It's one of the reasons I have a fierce fight inside me to stand up for the underdog, for those who get pushed around and bullied. If I could do ninth grade over again, I would stay. I would be a better friend to a couple of kids who forty-some years ago rescued me from the pain of exclusion.

A Human-Sized Hole

Here's the truth about all of us: We need friends. It's how God made us. There was a stretch not too long ago when I didn't have any close friends. I thought I didn't need them, so I golfed alone, hunted alone, and ate lunch at my desk alone. But I noticed that I was losing my passion for the things I used to love. Life wasn't fun anymore. *I* wasn't fun anymore. I was moody and increasingly afraid of what people were thinking and saying about me because I'd become isolated. It's part of what landed me in front of a counselor.

Today I'm a true believer—I need friends; it's one of my fundamental needs. Our need for friends is so deeply hardwired in us by God that we can't function without them. In fact, loneliness is the built-in signal for friendship just as hunger is the built-in signal for food, thirst is the built-in signal for water, and exhaustion is the built-in signal for rest. Loneliness is your soul telling you that you need to connect; it's a fundamental human need.

When God created the first man, Adam enjoyed a perfect friendship with God, but in spite of that friendship, God said, "It is not good for man to be alone." It's the only negative thing God ever said about his creation. Inside every human being is a God-sized hole that no human can fill, but there's also a human-sized hole that even God doesn't fill. If either is empty, we'll feel the pain of loneliness.

I think a student's greatest worry is not grades, money, or even a job; it's whether they have any friends. A stay-at-home mom's greatest concern is not whether the kids will behave but whether she'll have anyone to talk to or go to lunch with. Even a business-person whose life has been about making deals will eventually desire real friends with whom to share his life.

A few years ago, *Chicago Tribune* columnist Marla Paul wrote about how lonely she was feeling.[3] After people read her column, they stopped her at work, at the store, and at her daughter's school. "You too?" people marveled. "I thought I was the only one." Let-ters poured in from homemakers and CEOs. The column drew seven times the usual number of emails, and they all had the same theme: Why do I feel so lonely?

I think there are three common forms of loneliness.

Situational loneliness happens to all of us. It's when you're not chosen for the team, or it's a Friday night and the phone doesn't ring, or it's your birthday and no one remembers, or you just feel lonely for no reason at all. That's life. Everyone experiences situ-ational loneliness.

Seasonal loneliness is when you go off to college, or you move, or your friend moves, or a parent dies. It's the pit-in-your-stomach kind of loneliness that lasts for a season. Again, this is normal, and it happens to all of us.

Chronic loneliness is deeper and needs attention. It can be brought on by divorce, the death of a loved one, a severe loss, or lifelong rejection. Chronic loneliness can morph into other is-sues like depression, hopelessness, and even thoughts of suicide. Chronic loneliness is a signal that professional intervention may be needed.

I'm quite certain that my need for friends borders on a neurosis. If I sense that someone doesn't like me as much as I thought, my spirit sags a little. Sometimes I get the feeling that only my dog truly likes me. She's lying at my feet while I write this, looking up at me with two long drools hanging out of her mouth because she's waiting to lick the bottom of my coffee cup. She's also somewhat neurotic, which is why we like each other.

Fringe Benefits

Proverbs 17:17 says, "A friend loves at all times." Do you have anyone who loves you at all times? If you do, you are uniquely blessed. No other factor has a greater impact on your happiness, physical health, and success. John Ortberg asserts that nobody fails at love and succeeds at life, and nobody succeeds at love and fails at life.[4]

A true friend loves you *at all times*. Not because you are perfect, not because you are never grumpy, arrogant, or selfish. They love you at all times because they need you as much as you need them, and you're both willing to overlook faults and forgive each other because that's what all friendships require.

My daughter, Meg, and her friend Vanessa have been best friends since first grade. When I asked them what's held their friendship together all these years, Meg said, "We just get each other. We have the same values, same faith, same church, same school. She's my oldest friend. We laugh together, and we just get each other."

When you find someone in this world who has seen you at your worst but loves you anyway, hang on to that person, because a friendship like that happens only once or twice in a lifetime. When you have a friend who loves you at all times, you can face the world.

Proverbs says that there are two main benefits to having a few good friends.

Two Are Better Than One

Proverbs 27:10 says, "Do not forsake your friend or a friend of your family. . . . Better a neighbor nearby than a relative far away." Who can you call on to help you when you need an extra hand? My neighbors have helped me hold a ladder, carry things into my house, fix my cars, and skin a deer. My brother lives in California—he's not around. "Better a neighbor nearby than a relative far away." A friend is as valuable as family, sometimes more.

Bill Butters has been a loyal friend for twenty-two years. Bill played hockey in the NHL and was better known for fighting than his hockey skills. He's been a coach for the University of Minnesota and Wisconsin hockey teams, but his main passion is to help young men find new life through a relationship with Jesus Christ.

One day Bill and I decided to take a thirty-mile bike ride together, which worried me because Bill bikes a lot. He's a beast of a man, and the last thing a strong athlete wants is a wimpy little preacher boy holding him back.

We started out, and we were riding at a pace I knew I couldn't sustain, but I thought as long as Bill blocked the wind, maybe I could make it. I stayed with him for three or four miles, but I was fading fast. So I thought, "How can we do this together so that Bill gets his workout and I don't die?" There was only one solution. Grab hold of his shorts and let him tow me for long intervals. When I grabbed his shorts, he turned to me and said softly, "That's okay. That's what Debbie [his wife] does when we roller blade together." That's nice.

In Ecclesiastes, Solomon writes, "Two are better than one. . . . If either of them falls down, one can help the other up. But pity anyone who falls and has no one to help them up" (4:9–10). Because of all the fighting and blows Bill took to his head in the NHL, he's now prone to seizures. When his first seizure hit and the paramedics rolled him out of his house, I was able to be there to pray with Bill, and I could see the gratitude in his eyes when he saw me at his side. That's why he lets me grab his shorts—we pick each other up when the other one falls.

Who's there to pick you up when you fall? Who are your "2 a.m. friends" whom you could call for any reason and they'd come to your aid? Your 2 a.m. crisis is coming, and it's better to have a friend nearby than a relative far away.

Strong Friends Make You Stronger

Proverbs 27:17 says, "As iron sharpens iron, so one person sharpens another." You need some friends in your life who are strong enough to sharpen you and challenge you to become better.

I was walking up the fairway with my friend Trent when I said something flippant about another golfer whom we'd met earlier and who was on the course somewhere behind us. Lovingly but firmly Trent said, "You need to stop doing that."

I said, "What?"

"Talking so negatively and loudly about people; you offend more people than you know."

Not many people have the courage and strength to do that for me.

At first when he said it, I wanted to kick his ball out of bounds and cough loudly on his backswing. I didn't like him telling me that. I wanted to defend myself and tell him that he's no gem, but I knew he was right, and I was embarrassed. Finally, I said, "You're right. I've gotta work on that."

Trent makes me better because his metal is strong enough to make an impact. And he's good at it. He asks questions like, "What would you say is your greatest weakness?" When I answer him, he says, "I struggle with that too—we should work on that." I know he's using psychobabble to sharpen me, but the way he goes about it somehow makes it seem okay, like a dentist who says, "You'll feel a little pinch" while he's sticking a three-inch needle into your gum.

Which of your friends are strong enough to make you stronger and sharper?

It's not overreaching to say that the quality of your friends determines the quality of your life. Through extensive research on friendships, Tom Rath found that having a few vital friends actually decreases our risk for heart disease and even affects our diet.[5] Rath found that if your best friend has a healthy diet, you are five times more likely to have a healthy diet as well.[6]

Rath also mentions a study at Duke University that found nothing impacts our ability to thrive physically and psychologically more than having a few vital friends, and nothing impedes our ability to thrive more than lacking vital friends or when the quality of our friends is low.[7] Rick Warren says, "Nothing sabotages a person's life as quickly as wrong relationships."[8]

How are you doing in the friendship category? Would you answer yes or no to the following questions?

Do I have a friend I can call even at 2 a.m.? NO

Is there someone who could accurately name my greatest fears and weaknesses? NO

Do I have one or more friends whom I meet with regularly? NO

If I received good news, such as a promotion, do I have a friend I would call immediately just to let them know? NO

If this person was not around, would the quality of my life and happiness go down significantly? YeS

Do we experience mutual joy when we see each other?[9] ?

If you can't answer yes to most of these questions, you may need to join a small group or invite someone to coffee as a first step toward friendship.

How to Find Wise Friendships

Go for Less

The most perfect example of human life, Jesus, had twelve close friends, and of those twelve he had a special bond with three, Peter, James, and John. Even the perfect Son of God couldn't maintain more than twelve friendships.

The truth is that you will have either lots of shallow acquaintances or a few close friends. It's easy to fall for quantity over quality, but that's a mistake, because research and experience prove that having a few close friends is what makes for a happy and successful life. No one has enough time to maintain more than a dozen good friendships and two or three really close friendships. That means you have to prune away some dead-end relationships and say no to what could be some potential good friendships.

In her book *Bittersweet*, Shauna Niequist writes about her home team.

Everybody has a home team: it's the people you call when you get a flat tire or when something terrible happens. It's the people who, near or far, know everything that's wrong with you and love you anyway. . . . It's so easy to give everything we have to the first people

114

who ask, or the people who ask the most often, or the people who are always in crisis. But stop yourself: are they a part of your home team? . . . There is a totally finite amount of time and energy that each of us have to give to the people in our lives. You can give yours to your home team. Or you can spend it haphazardly on an odd collection of people who need something from you, largely because you don't want to say no.[10]

When I read that, I immediately wrote down eighteen people who are on my home team; they're the ones in my speed dial. The first person on my home team is my wife, followed by my kids, my mom, my brother, my sisters, and a few in-laws. I also have some staff people in there and a couple others.

People who boast about having eight hundred Facebook friends are delusional—and often lonely. Meg Jay reports that many of her twentysomething clients secretly hate Facebook because people post their most glorious moments and leave out their mundane ones, which makes viewers wonder why their own lives are so lousy.[11]

Facebook fanatics get sucked into the false notion that more is better. More is not better; it's not even real. Jay says Facebook is "just another place, not to be, but to *seem*."[12] One of Jay's clients confessed that every time somebody on Facebook changes their status from single to engaged or married, she panics. "I'm convinced Facebook was invented to make single people feel bad about their lives."[13]

The truth is that life has far more ordinary days than perfect days, and the key to turning ordinary days into good days is to cultivate a few close friendships and let go of the rest.

Proverbs 18:24 says, "One who has unreliable friends soon comes to ruin, but there is a friend who sticks closer than a brother." Don't ruin your life by trying to keep up with people who don't even care about you that much. Rather, invest in a few friends who will stick closer to you than a brother. Go for less.

Look Closer to Home

Your best chances at finding wise friends are close to home. There are exceptions—not everyone who's in close proximity to you is wise, but your best potential friends are not "out there some-where." They're in your church, school, and neighborhood. My best friends don't live out of state, because friendships require face time. Proximity matters.

For many years, I made the mistake of thinking that if looked long enough I'd eventually find the perfect set of friends. So I with-held my friendship from certain people because they had a flaw, quirk, or annoyance that I didn't like. I reasoned, "I'm not gonna invest in this person because I might miss out on someone better who comes along." Consequently, I missed out on some really great friendships in high school, college, and beyond.

In my first book, I mentioned the moment I looked around the room at our leadership meeting, leaned back in my chair, and had what could be described as an epiphany, a lightning bolt of clarity. I thought:

> Every one of these people has flaws, something that annoys me. But these are some of the best people in the world—it really doesn't get any better than this. Bob, what lifetime are you waiting for? You can either come to work day after day, week after week thinking that there's a better group of people somewhere out there, or you can start to invest in and enjoy the ones God has put right under your nose.[14]

I also sensed God's Spirit saying, "Bob, you think *they* have flaws. You're no picnic. How would you like to be them and have to try to get along with you? Wake up before it's too late."

So I made a conscious decision right there in that meeting that these were the people I wanted to do life with, and I actually told them that, and it's made a huge difference. Now we visit one an-other's offices, eat together, travel together, pray for and laugh with one another. It's like someone turned on a switch that changed my whole attitude about friends at work. Our work environment used to be toxic and friendship averse. No longer.

These days we put a high value on building relational capital, and we actually insist on it. We talk about it in staff meetings. We intentionally laugh more, joke more, and spend more time with one another. When we do have conflicts—as all friends do—we're much quicker to patch things up because the friendship is now more important than any program or problem. We've grown to love one another with what Paul describes as "genuine affection" (Romans 12:10 NLT).

By the way, relatives count. Laurie is my best friend. I love being with her, coming home to her, and watching sports with her. Marriage expert Les and Leslie Parrott write, "The emotional intimacy a married couple shares is said to be five times more important than their physical intimacy."[15] I'd say it's more like only *three* times as important, but a friendship with your spouse counts. When your marriage is working the way God intended, your home team is pretty much set and there's not a lot of loneliness. It takes about twenty years to work through the conflicts, being poor, learning each other's rhythms, and raising kids, but it's worth it. Marriage is amazing when you finally push through the hard years and you're able to become true friends.

Don't Expect One Person to Meet All Your Friendship Needs

Some people want one person to meet all their friendship needs, but that's impossible, whether it's a dating relationship, marriage, or friendship.

For example, your husband can be a great friend, but don't make him be your girlfriend; he doesn't care about what happens with the Kardashians. And husbands shouldn't expect their wives to be their male friends. I would never ruin a perfectly good hunting trip by bringing my wife along; she'd hate it, and so would I.

One person cannot meet all your friendship needs. Each of your friends will bring something different. Here's a key component to finding wise friends: focus on the positive aspects someone brings to the friendship, not on what they don't bring.

I have friends who energize me, encourage me, and challenge me.

I have friends who are good at hunting, fishing, and tying knots and others who are good at praying, advising, and mentoring.

Another key is this: What do *you* bring to the friendship? A mistake I've made is to evaluate a potential friendship based solely on what the other person can do for me. Will they be fun for me, will they be interesting, energetic, and good for me?

This is incredibly selfish, and it pushes people away because I'm expecting others to carry the relational load. I've learned that it's not enough for me just to show up and grace people with my charming presence; I have to bring some energy and effort to the friendship and share the relational load. Friendships require give-and-take.

They also need room to breathe. A friendship has to have enough flexibility and trust so that friends can go several weeks or even months without a phone call and still be okay. Nobody has it all or can give it all, so don't expect it.

Address Your Relational Viruses

Proverbs 22:24 says, "Do not make friends with a hot-tempered person." Henry Cloud says, "You just don't see people who are successful in life who are hotheads."[16] Neither are they addicts, needy, whiny, jokesters, self-absorbed, or pushy. Eventually, those things damage relationships and push people away, at least people who could be a wise friend.

What's the one thing about you that hurts your friendships? If you don't know, ask your spouse or friends. If you have kids, ask them; they'll tell you because they're the recipients of it. People who are dishonest, addicted, or immoral are not friendship material, and healthy people know it. If you don't have many or any friends, or if you're always in conflict, solicit some feedback from a counselor or someone who cares about you because you may have a relational virus that pushes potential friends away.

Meatball Friends

My wife makes the best meatball spaghetti sauce in the world, and the secret is the quality of the meat and the quantity of the heat. She finds the best and leanest ground chuck, adds her special ingredients to the meat, and then drops them raw into a huge pot of Prego spaghetti sauce. Prego is iffy at best, but when the whole thing cooks and simmers all day long, the meatballs become a part of the sauce and the sauce becomes a part of the meatballs, producing a flavor and tenderness that make most Italian restaurants a disappointment to me.

Here's what I've learned. When it comes to friends, it's the quality of the meat and the quantity of the heat.

You can't go to find-a-friend.com and expect quality. You can't get into the same pot with just any old meatball. If your friends are filled with impurities such as dishonesty, selfishness, greed, impure thoughts, and dirty speech, and you're in the same pot with them at school, the bar, the nightclub, or the fraternity or sorority, then you're going to have bad sauce. That stuff will leak into your life and sabotage any chance for a wise friendship.

Could you be a positive influence on them? Yes, but only if the power and purity of Christ are strong enough in you to overcome their poor qualities. We're all called to be a positive influence on people who perhaps aren't friendship quality yet, but that's often more of a ministry than a friendship. It's important to understand the difference between trying to minister to someone and forming a true friendship. Don't make the mistake of taking on so many projects that you don't have room for true friendships. Even Jesus pulled away from the crowd to be alone with his true friends.

Once you find quality friends, you need to add heat. You have to have enough simmer time together so that your life begins to permeate your friends' lives and their lives begin to permeate and flavor yours. There's no shortcut; you can't microwave quality friendships.

So whom do you simmer with? Who are your meatball friends? Because the quality of your friends will determine the quality of your life. Find a few good meatballs and make life taste great!

10

Wise Revenge

Do not say, "I'll pay you back for this wrong!"
Wait for the LORD, and he will avenge you.

Proverbs 20:22

Chairs and Acorns

Several years ago, my wife and I attended Marketfest, an evening festival held in our small town of White Bear Lake. We went to watch our daughter and her friends put on a show with their gymnastics team. About an hour before the girls performed, we began looking for a place to sit.

I did a quick scan and was amazed to see two unoccupied chairs not too far from us, so we quickly walked toward them. The problem was that sitting between those two empty chairs was a man who had an arm wrapped around the chair on either side of him as if to say to any intruder, "Don't even think about it."

Ignoring his nonverbal cue, I politely leaned over and said, "Are these taken?"

"Yes!" he said abruptly and looked away.

Just as I was about to say, "By whom?" I felt my arm being yanked out of its socket by my wife as she tried to pull me away. Knowing that I don't go down easily, she said in a forceful whisper, "Bob, let it go."

"But look at him," I shot back. "The place is jammed, and he's sitting there like he owns those chairs; let me just ask him if we can sit until his party comes back."

She said, "Let it go."

Just then a miracle happened; two chairs opened up directly behind this guy, and we quickly sat down. For the next forty-five minutes, we watched person after person walk up to him and ask if those two chairs were taken. And for forty-five minutes, without hesitation or shame, he clung to those chairs. I sat behind him with my arms crossed. I'd completely forgotten all about the gymnastics because I was doing a slow burn trying not to lose my Christianity.

Finally, two elderly women limped up to him—this is the honest truth, one even had a cane. They politely asked if the two chairs were taken, and with a cold, stone heart, he snipped, "Yes, they're taken," and he looked away.

"That's it," I said to Laurie.

She said, "Bob, remember who you are."

Finally, another man came along, a man I knew who frankly didn't deserve a chair, and sat down next to him. They never did use the other chair.

I was fuming. When we got up to leave, I noticed an acorn on the ground—an acorn I'm convinced was placed there by God. I picked it up, and the question was to flick or not to flick. Laurie, who sometimes sounds like the Holy Spirit, said, "Bob!" Then she added, "What would Jesus do?"

"I think he'd flick."

I didn't really think that, but isn't it amazing how quickly things can go south, how in a matter of minutes I could go from being carefree to being angry, hateful, and wanting to bean a complete stranger with an acorn?

Clearly this guy was a selfish dolt who needed a good beaning, but what about me? I piled up a whole stack of sins, without even trying, against some random guy at Marketfest.

And those are just little sins that I'm willing to confess in a book. I've had worse things happen in my marriage; we've gone days without speaking to each other over stupid stuff. Battle lines get drawn, things get said, and all we can think of is how to get back at the person who wronged us.

Sin and revenge are what land people who once loved each other in front of a judge. It's what blows families apart, divides neighbors, causes lawsuits, and leads to fights and even murder. It's why schools and cities aren't safe and why every night when we turn on the television we see people firing assault weapons and lobbing mortars at one another. Why? Because someone crossed a line. Somebody took something, said something, or did something that wasn't fair, and now they're going to pay.

Bold Revenge

Revenge comes from an ingrained sense of fairness. Parents don't have to teach little kids how to demand fairness; it rises up naturally. Fairness is a natural human expectation. And when something isn't fair, we get angry and want to even the score. We want revenge.

The Bible teaches that there's a place for anger and revenge. Scripture does not call us to be spineless pushovers who never speak up or take a stand. Look what Solomon says about justice and revenge.

> When justice is done, it brings joy to the righteous.
> (Prov. 21:15)
> It will go well with those who convict the guilty.
> (Prov. 24:25)
> Speak up for those who cannot speak for themselves.
> (Prov. 31:8)
> Defend the rights of the poor and needy. (Prov. 31:9)

Nothing angers us more than when those who lie, cheat, steal, and abuse get away with it, because it strikes at our sense of fairness—right and wrong. It angers God too. Proverbs 17:15 says, "Acquitting the guilty and condemning the innocent—the LORD detests them both."

God hates it when the guilty go free and the innocent are left holding the bag. And if God hates it, so should we. There's nothing wrong with being angry at injustice; we *should* be angry—the Bible teaches that the guilty should pay and the innocent should be protected.

When I was a senior in high school, we were running off the field after football practice, and I heard laughing and screaming behind me. I looked back and saw two of my senior teammates picking on a sophomore, literally trying to rip his pants off in front of some cheerleaders. I knew these guys, and I knew it was not the time to say, "Now, boys, we shouldn't rip the pants off of sophomores." But I remembered reading Psalm 82:3: "Defend the weak."

I was just 155 pounds, but I was fast, and I knew how to hit. I sprinted toward my two senior teammates who were 185 pounds each, lowered my shoulder, and hit one of them chest high at full speed. He sat on his butt dazed. Then he looked at me and said, "What'd you do that for?"

I said, "I'm defending the cause of the weak." My leadership style was a little abrasive back then, but that hit put a stop to hazing that year.

A Good Word Gone Bad

We live in a world where it seems as though criminals sometimes have more rights than victims, where protecting a person's right to express himself is more important than the law. I'm sorry, but terrorists, pedophiles, looters, and abusers have forfeited their rights, and to suggest otherwise is irresponsible. Yet we're admonished to be tolerant of all people, withhold judgment, and be sympathetic toward their values no matter how destructive they are.

Nonsense!

Tolerance used to mean that we would debate our differences in a civil, respectful manner. Today tolerance means that we must accept all viewpoints no matter how wrong or destructive, that everyone's opinion is morally equal. Today's form of tolerance has erased the line between good and evil. This is completely opposed to the heart of God.

English writer Dorothy Sayers describes it well:

> Tolerance is the sin which believes nothing, cares for nothing, interferes with nothing, loves nothing, hates nothing, finds purpose in nothing, lives for nothing, stands for nothing, and only remains alive because there is nothing it would die for.[1]

Today's tolerance asks us to disengage our brain and ignore our moral conscience. But it's never right to tolerate physical abuse. It's never right to tolerate the exploitation of children. It's never loving or right to tolerate adultery, bullying, or theft. The Bible teaches, and common sense affirms, that these are immoral acts that deserve retribution. Dan Allender says, "The desire for revenge is far from being a merely fallen human emotion; it is a reflection of the purest longing for justice."[2]

If you get angry over abuse, if your insides churn over injustice, if you long for good to be rewarded and for evil to be punished, that means you're spiritually alive. The desire for revenge is triggered by a longing for justice and grows out of our intrinsic sense of goodness.

But what is wise revenge?

Wise revenge is discerning. It knows when to demand justice and when to extend mercy. Its ultimate goal is to right wrongs, restore goodness, and overcome evil.

Wise revenge realizes that we live in a fallen world where we could spend every day trying to get even with someone who wronged us—driving to work, in the checkout line, at the dinner table, on the soccer field, at the airport, on Facebook. The list of those who fail us and hurt us is endless, and if our goal is to exact revenge every time we're wronged, we'll spend our entire life doing so.

That's not wise.

Wise Revenge Lives in the Balance of Tenderness and Strength

Wise revenge understands that relationships are complex and require different responses for different offenses. Relationships that work best are made up of people who can discern what's needed more, tenderness or strength. And often we have to discern the right mix while in midsentence.

I have at times been in sharp disagreements with my wife, kids, or colleagues at work and have had a momentary flash of discernment that tells me to throttle back and inject some tenderness. I wish it happened more often, but it might be a tender phrase, smile, or tone in my voice that completely turns the conversation from being adversarial to congenial.

Other times the relationship requires strength, and you have to launch yourself helmet first into the chest of your teammate. Or get a lawyer, restraining order, or new phone number.

Appropriate revenge is found somewhere between tenderness and strength, between justice and mercy, and its ultimate goal is not to punish but to restore—to right wrongs, restore goodness, and offer a chance at new life.

Appropriate revenge asks the question, "What does love require here?"

What does love require when . . .

my teammate bullies a younger player?

my friend cheats on an exam?

my colleague is dishonest with me?

my father wants to reconcile with me?

my son says that he's homosexual?

my spouse confesses an affair to me?

Sometimes love requires tenderness, other times strength. Often it's a mixture of both.

Wise Revenge Leaves Room for God's Wrath

King Solomon reflects on all the relationships he's had in life, including with his political enemies, internal rebels, merchants and craftsmen who may have overcharged him, wives and concubines who may have cheated on him, and this is what he concludes: "Do not say, 'I'll pay you back for this wrong!' Wait for the LORD, and he will avenge you" (Prov. 20:22).

Three insights emerge here.

People Are Going to Disappoint You

Solomon assumes that you and I will be wronged. Expect it. Don't be surprised by it. The sooner you understand that the world is filled with sinful, flawed people who offend, irritate, and hurt one another, the less derailed you'll be when it happens. Eventually, your parent will disappoint you, your spouse will offend you, and your friend will let you down. If you have a teenager, they will likely wreck your car, break curfew, or lie to you. Prepare yourself so that when it happens you won't flip out. Sinful people do sinful things.

Solomon Encourages a Spirit of Benevolence

Don't say, "I'll pay you back for this wrong."

Some people have a fist-pounding, vindictive spirit that says, "I'm going to get you back no matter how long it takes," and that becomes their obsession in life, preventing them from moving forward. Solomon says, "Let it go; cultivate a benevolent spirit. It's easier on your heart and your home."

Solomon Encourages a Deep Trust in God That He Will Handle It

"Wait for the LORD, and he will avenge you." In his letter to the Romans, Paul echoes Solomon's wisdom and says, "Do not take revenge, my dear friends, but leave room for God's wrath, for it is written: 'It is mine to avenge; I will repay,' says the Lord" (12:19).

Most of us don't want to wait for the Lord; we don't want to leave room for God's wrath for two reasons: (1) we want the satisfaction of inflicting the pain ourselves, and (2) we don't think God will actually come through. But the Bible promises, "God will repay."

The very day I wrote this section, the sanctions against Penn State University were handed down by the NCAA violations board for the gross negligence in the 2012 child abuse case. The night before, the nine-hundred-pound bronze statue of Coach Joe Paterno was removed from the entrance of Beaver Stadium, where Joe coached his teams to 409 wins—an NCAA record. Joe was the winningest coach in college football and was revered by those who knew him.

I met Coach Paterno once. I was cutting through a back alley on my way to class when I looked over and there was the legendary coach walking through a parking lot. I decided not to bother him but then thought, "Nuts to that. That's Joe Paterno. I'm gonna meet him."

I ran over and quickly introduced myself. He stopped, smiled, and said, "What are you studying here, Bob?" When I told him, he said, "Good luck, and nice meeting you." Joe was a class act, a family man who was devoted to his faith. He gave millions to charity and to Penn State.

I remember watching his life unravel on television and thinking, "Eighty-eight years—successful, loved, famous, wealthy, a legend of historic proportions. And in a span of months, it was all dust."

Paterno was fired, Sandusky was given life in prison, Paterno died, his family was disgraced, and Penn State football received a fatal blow—fined $60 million, banned from postseason play for four years, eighty scholarships revoked over four years that will devastate the program, and all wins (111) from 1998 to 2011 revoked, dropping the famed coach from first to eighth.

Instead of being known as a great football tradition led by a once-revered man, Penn State and Joe Paterno will forever be associated with the awful abuse of children.

Solomon warns, "Do not fret because of evildoers or be envious of the wicked, for the evildoer has no future hope, and the lamp of the wicked will be snuffed out" (Prov. 24:19–20). He then says in Proverbs 29:1 that evil people will "suddenly be destroyed." This is the pattern of the wicked—their demise happens slowly, and then all at once.

For fifteen years, a dozen or more young boys lived with the pain and shame of their abuse while their tormentor went free. For fifteen years, nothing was done, nothing was said, everything was hidden and left unpunished. Sometimes revenge happens slowly, painfully slowly, and then suddenly the gavel falls, God's wrath is released, and justice wins. In three months' time, their lamp was snuffed out.

I don't know what kind of wrongs you've had to endure. Some of you have had to endure unspeakable things that deserve criminal prosecution. Others of us have fared better, but sooner or later everyone gets hurt, everyone gets wronged and cheated.

Wise revenge leaves room for God's wrath. It releases the person who hurt you into God's hands for his perfect judgment. It understands that God is just and that in the end his justice will win. "I will repay," says the Lord.

It's a matter of trusting him who never broke a promise.

Wise Revenge Puts a Higher Value on Relationship than on Revenge

The Need for Forgiveness

Wise revenge understands that relationships are not possible without forgiveness. All of us are sinners. All of us are flawed. I hurt you and you hurt me, which means that our only hope for a relationship is forgiveness. And forgiveness means that I must be willing to suspend revenge for the sake of the relationship. I must, at times, be willing to be wronged, offended, or hurt if I want to have relationships. If my supreme goal is to get even, then I'll be alone in life, because relationships can't survive by constantly getting even. Somebody has to be mature enough to put a higher value on relationship than revenge, and that requires forgiveness.

The truth is that forgiveness isn't fair. Revenge is fair, getting even is fair, but forgiveness isn't fair. Philip Yancey captures the unfairness of forgiveness in his book *What's So Amazing about Grace*:

[My wife and I] were discussing my shortcomings in a rather spirited way when she said, "I think it's pretty amazing that I forgave you of some of the dastardly things you've done." Forgiveness is achingly difficult, and even after you've forgiven, the wound—my dastardly deeds—live on in memory. Forgiveness is an unnatural act, and my wife was simply protesting its blatant unfairness.[3]

Forgiveness is always hard because it *isn't* fair, and it doesn't erase the memory or the hurt. It's also confusing, so let's be clear about what forgiveness is not.

Forgiveness does not mean you have to trust the person who hurt you, because some people are toxic and destructive, and if they keep hurting you, you need to tell them, "I can forgive you. I can suspend revenge, but I cannot trust you. I need distance from you."

Forgiveness does not mean you have to forget. People say you should "forgive and forget," but I've never been able to do that. In fact, I think it can be irresponsible to forget because you could foolishly subject yourself to repeat patterns of manipulation and abuse.

Forgiveness does not mean reconciliation—that you have to restore the relationship. Reconciliation is a two-way street that requires healthy change in both parties. If the other person continues to be hurtful and dishonest, they are not relationship material. They have work to do with a professional counselor in order to become relationally healthy. Pulling away from them may be what God uses to get them to address their sin.

Finally, forgiveness is not immediate. It is not an event. Forgiveness is usually a process that can take years, and it often has starts and stops. You may have forgiven someone and suspended revenge temporarily only to find that you're mad and vengeful all over again. You may have to forgive someone over and over until one day you realize that God has replaced your seething anger with genuine care. Time and distance help.

Think before You Speak

One of the reasons revenge is so dangerous for me is because my perspective is usually clouded by my own sin. There is almost never a time when my judgment is perfectly accurate, because it's muddled by greed, anger, and selfishness. The truth is that I can't trust myself because of the insidious effect that selfishness has on my motives. Am I yelling at my kids because they did something wrong or because I accepted too many commitments and my patience is thin? Did I snap at my wife because she bought another useless coupon book or magazine subscription from one of the dozen fund-raisers who come knocking at our door every fall or because I'm penny-pinching for a new set of clubs?

Sometimes I'll get an email at work that flat-out angers me. Someone takes a swipe at me for something I said in a sermon or questions my wisdom because of a decision I made, and instantly I feel my body react—my jaw tenses up and my fingers start to shake. My immediate response is to get revenge, tell them off, and set them straight. I want to inflict pain on them. To quote my daughter, "I want to poke their eyes out." She's plagued by the same disease as I am.

Why do I want revenge? Because I'm weak. I'm immature. My judgment is clouded by arrogance and ego. I think too highly of myself and that I'm above criticism. Arrogance is dangerous because it prevents us from seeing our flaws; it skews our judgment.

The most dangerous moment for me is when I first see the email, because I have this surge of emotion and anger. If I respond in the moment, I end up saying things that are destructive and will diminish my credibility and hurt the relationship.

So here's what I do. First, I never respond right away. I sit on the email, sometimes for several days. Once I've calmed down, I reread it and try to find the kernels of truth tucked inside the criticism. Then I challenge myself to try to win my critic over by being gracious.

Sometimes I'll get an email that's completely hateful and doesn't warrant a response. Other times I'll hear from a fanatic who has a theological agenda that's so far off the grid that I don't respond. But if it's a straight criticism, even if I think they're wrong, I now begin every response with the following:

Dear ____,

Thank you for taking the time to write.

I always thank them because they invested some time and cared enough to raise their concern. Far better to have a critic write to you than have them spew venom behind your back.

When my first book was published, I told a story in a sermon about going to Nashville to meet my literary agent. The reason I told this story was because I lost my cell phone in the airport, which cascaded into a series of mishaps that injected humor and made for a good point. The following Wednesday morning I received an email from Bill.

Pastor:

As a regular online listener to your sermons, I most often times find your perspectives on Scripture both informative and persuasive. I attribute much of your impact on the sort of "common man" persona projected by the experiences you often recount. It's as if I were listening to the sage advice of a trusted friend on my front porch.

But your book writing pursuit has changed that, at least occasionally now. You seem intent on speaking to us from a loftier perch. Certainly traveling to Nashville could be referenced, but to broadcast the purpose of the trip "to see my literary agent" strikes me as bragging, which for what it's worth, I don't let my friends get away with on my porch.

There are people in your fold who don't have $20 for gas in their car, much less money for a far-flung trip to talk up one's bookwriting credentials in the company of an agent. Insolent sports figures have agents. Pastors should have "helpers" or "guides" or "advisors," and really good pastors like you should have the wise counsel of a wife, who, with red pen in hand, strike from the prepared text these lapses in good judgment.

Sincerely,

Bill

Not a rip-roaring criticism, but along with his compliments (which I tend not to hear), I think he accused me of being a braggart, being insolent, and lacking in judgment, and maybe that I could have married better. So I closed the email to let my emotions subside, opened it the next day, and challenged myself to make a friend. I wrote:

Hey, Bill,

Thanks for listening and taking the time to write. I take your points well and never want to come across as pompous or arrogant; I apologize if referencing a literary agent sounded like bragging. I didn't mean for it to sound that way. The only reason I mentioned it, and I mean ONLY, is for the story I extracted about losing my phone.

With that said, my messages are scrutinized by a team of eight people with "red pen" in hand before I ever speak. I never speak a message without the editing eyes of many others for the very reason you mentioned.

Again, I'm so sorry it struck you the way it did, and I will use your criticism to try to keep getting better at what I do. So thanks. And don't be a stranger; come and see us live—the music and people you'll encounter are far better than any of my messages.

Warmly,

Bob

Here are three things I've learned. First, critics often don't expect a response, and if they get one, it's usually vengeful. So honor them with a response and surprise them with humility. Sometimes that's all it takes to diffuse a potential battle.

Second, own what you can own. To Bill, my story sounded pompous and offensive. I have to own that. If that's how it came across to him, that's my fault; I have to validate and own that even if it wasn't my intention. In almost every criticism I get, no matter how vindictive, there's usually a nugget of truth that will help me get better.

Third, don't patronize or insult the critic's intelligence by completely caving in. I gave him enough facts to help fill in the gaps that were missing for him.

This is what Bill wrote back:

Pastor:

I so appreciate your response. I tend to be critical and quick to spot the speck in my neighbor's eye while I happily contend, unknowingly, with a plank in my own. Frankly, I should be in the lumber business.

My hope is for your church to reach deep into the abyss of apathy in our community. Every tortured soul you interrupt for Good is one less neighbor threatening my kids, stealing my bike, or cursing my wife's driving.

I love your brake job story. Let's one day find a pickup bumper to sit on and share a few minutes of life together.

Bill

Think of the damage I would have caused had I responded to Bill with revenge—lost credibility, tarnished reputation of our church, ammunition for him to use against me with his friends, and a lost opportunity to have influence in Bill's life and family. It took me five minutes to write that email. I'm hoping the payoff will be eternal.

Wise revenge puts a higher value on relationship than on revenge. It doesn't dwell so much on who people are but on who they could become if Christ entered their lives. Just think if the person you struggle with the most became loving, generous, kind, and good.

People can change. I've seen it happen. Before you take revenge, be wise. Put a higher value on the relationship than on revenge and see what God will do.

FAMILY
WISDOM

11

Wise Beginning

The fear of the LORD is the beginning of knowledge.

Proverbs 1:7

It's Super Bowl Sunday 2013, 5 degrees above zero back home, but I'm writing this chapter on a back patio in Palm Springs overlooking a private spa and pool. A family in our church gave us the keys to their winter home for ten days and said, "Enjoy." I was able to step away from work because our staff members are some of the best in the nation and will lead well in my absence. Yesterday I sat on the edge of the spa like a turtle warming himself in the sun. I took a bite of my turkey sandwich and said to Laurie, "I couldn't be more blessed. What God has done in our family and church is beyond my wildest dreams." What some people don't realize, however, is that my "turkey sandwich moment" is the result of a wise beginning that happened thirty-four years ago.

A Rough Start

If you're tempted to skip this chapter because you think that ship has sailed, let me ask you: do you have children, friends, co-workers who still have a shot at a wise beginning? Do you have a chance at a new beginning down the road when you are healed and healthy? Stick with me.

Thirty-four years ago, I sat across the table from a twenty-one-year-old girl at the Freight House Restaurant in Youngstown, Ohio. She was a senior at Grove City College in northwest Pennsylvania, and I was about to ask her if she'd spend the rest of her life with me. I remember my hand sweating while I clutched the little box in my pocket that contained a small diamond ring. There was nothing romantic about the Freight House, and who thinks about getting engaged in Youngstown? I could have picked Pittsburgh, the Poconos, or Slippery Rock Creek (my favorite trout stream)—anywhere but Youngstown.

But there we sat, and it was the biggest decision of our lives, because we both knew there was no turning back. Whom you marry will affect every part of your life for the rest of your life. As I sat looking across the table at this twenty-one-year-old Irish-Catholic girl and she sat looking at this kid with shoulder-length hair, we both knew this would be the best or worst decision of our lives. So I sweated and brooded. Laurie remembers it more like a job interview than an engagement. "Do you love Jesus? Could you ever be a pastor's wife? Could you ever live in Minnesota and be happy? Do you mind being poor? Can you cook wild game and like it?"

I painted about as real and depressing a picture as I could of what life would be like with me, because forever's a long time; you want to be as sure as you can.

I'm still a little amazed that she said yes, and when I gave her the ring, we didn't fawn all over each other, because now we had to tell people. I was immature and a little afraid, so I never asked her father for her hand in marriage. Instead, I drove her home from the Freight House, dropped her off in her driveway, and drove away as quickly as I could. The Thompsons were stunned. Laurie's sister Carolee took one look at Laurie's ring, stomped out of the room, and announced, "You're too young to get married." Her father was quiet, and her mother had a hard time being happy for her.

My parents were out of town, so I called them, and just before I hung up I quickly said, "Oh, by the way, Laurie and I got engaged tonight." There was silence on the other end and then a scream of anguish after my dad told my mom. So that went well.

The next year was a disaster filled with tension and arguments over all kinds of things related to money, moving, religious differences, and wedding plans. Our mothers were so distraught over our engagement that it made them both physically sick. My mom even wrote Laurie's mom a letter and told her to do whatever she could to get Laurie to break it off. We almost did twice, but the day of the wedding came, people smiled, pictures were taken, and families were cordial. But it was not the happiest day of our lives, and, consequently, our wedding album is the least-looked-at memento in our home.

Two weeks after our honeymoon, spent in second-rate campgrounds and nineteen-dollar-a-night roadside hotels along the East Coast, we packed all our possessions in a U-Haul and moved to St. Paul, Minnesota, where I enrolled in a summer Greek crash course to qualify for seminary. I barely passed. We slept on a mattress on the floor for a full year before we thought we could afford a bed frame. All I remember of our first year of marriage is going to class, being poor, and fighting over every little thing. The arguing and yelling were so bad that six months into the marriage we both concluded we'd married the wrong person.

But marriage is less about *finding* the right person and more about *becoming* the right person. I've met countless people who bailed on their marriage because after a few years of conflict they decided they'd married the wrong person. Or there's no chemistry. Or that "loving feeling" is gone.

Our loving feeling was so far gone that we never thought we'd love each other again. That's normal. It happens. Most young couples go through a season or two of intense conflict and fighting because they haven't worked through their expectations yet. They didn't know how annoying it can be to live with another person. Now they know.

But the answer isn't to quit. Anybody can quit. It takes people of strength and wisdom to say, "We've got a problem. But divorce isn't an option, so let's get some help and beat this thing."

All married people go through conflict and lose chemistry, but those are opportunities for you to evolve, grow, and change as a couple. Renew your friendship by getting away without the kids, see a counselor, or read a book on marriage together, because it is more about *becoming* the right person than *finding* the right person.

With that said, some people are *not* marriage material in their present state. I've tried to talk people out of divorce who are ready to end their marriage, but when I meet their spouse, I wonder, "What were you thinking?" The person I'm counseling seems normal and relatively healthy, but their spouse is a train wreck. It *is* less about finding the right person and more about becoming the right person, but don't marry a project, because what you see is what you get. Some people are simply not fit to be married as they are. Maya Angelou says, "When people show you who they are, believe them."[1] They need to take responsibility for whatever dysfunctions they have, get professional help, and become relationally healthy.

Lock the Exit Door

The one thing that saved Laurie and me was our commitment to stay married "for better or worse." We were in the middle of "worse," but our commitment was forever, no matter what. We vowed that the *D* word would never cross our lips even as a threat, so we locked the exit door and threw away the key. When you lock the exit door to marriage and throw away the key, your only option is to work it out. You say, "You're stuck with me and I'm stuck with you. Our only option is to find out what's wrong and get it fixed." Pastor Voddie Baucham tells his wife, "If you leave, I'm going with you."[2] That's the spirit.

Some of you might be right where we were and are tempted to call it quits. Every marriage has problems, but you don't solve them by walking away; you solve them by finding out what the problems are, getting some professional help, and changing bad behaviors. That's how you end up sitting on the edge of a spa eating a turkey sandwich thirty-four years later more in love with your wife than ever.

Nobody would have said that Laurie and I had a wise beginning, but it's what was below the surface that was important and that laid the foundation for a long, happy life together.

A Wise Beginning—Two Ingredients

Let me start by saying that second only to your decision to follow Christ is deciding whom you will marry. Get that right and you can handle the world; get it wrong and the world will handle you. When my marriage is good, I can handle just about any adversity that comes my way, but when my marriage is bad, I can't handle much of anything. And those who think that the saying "opposites attract" is a good thing are delusional. Having some opposite interests is fine and even healthy, but if you're opposite in your faith, morals, values, spending habits, and parenting philosophies, you're headed for trouble. The old adage is true: Opposites attract, but then they attack.

As I look back, I see two main ingredients that got us through those hard years and laid the foundation for our marriage, our family, and ultimately our entire life. There are no guarantees when it comes to marriage, but these two ingredients will help every couple have a wise beginning that leads to a long, happy life.

Genuine Faith in God

Through all our arguing and uncertainty during that first year, our faith in God was the one constant that held us together. Proverbs 1:7 says, "The fear of the LORD is the beginning of knowledge."

In chapter 1, I said that those who acquire wisdom generally end up acquiring honor, long life, and wealth—not just material wealth but wealth in the broadest sense of relational and spiritual well-being. Go after wisdom and you get wealth thrown in; go after wealth and you might not get anything.

The beginning of wisdom and a "wealthy" life is when we fear the Lord. Solomon doesn't mean we should be afraid of God but that we should revere God as the source of all wisdom, authority, and power. Fearing God means living every day with the awareness that God is in charge and that he's put us on the planet to live our lives according to his plan and purpose. It means that the smartest thing I can do is look toward heaven every day and say, "God, there is nothing more important in my life than knowing and following you. Lead me, fill me, and show me the way." Simply put, it's looking to God every day and inviting him to be at the center of your life. It's asking him to take his rightful place in your life and looking to his Word, the Bible, as the supreme authority in your decisions, family, and work.

Anyone who does that is a wise person, because they will make decisions based not on popular opinion or talk show advice but on God's eternal Word. Jesus said, "Seek *first* his kingdom and his righteousness, and all these things will be given to you as well" (Matt. 6:33, emphasis added). Put God and his kingdom first in your life, and all the things you stress about—money, work, school, relationships—will eventually fall into place because you've learned to do them God's way, not your way.

A wise beginning starts with faith in God, the fear of the Lord. At the beginning of our marriage, Laurie and I tried to keep God at the center of our lives, and that single value carried us through. Laurie often said to me, "Even though you were being stupid and unreasonable, I knew that your devotion to God would eventually bring you around."

Growing up, we both went to church. I went with my family; she went with hers. Even as a teenager, I was in church two or three times a week. I know that going to church doesn't automatically make someone a Christian, but that's where my spiritual foundation was formed—my moral and biblical nonnegotiables. God and church were as normal to me as going to school. For a lot of people today, God and church take second and third place to weekend soccer tournaments and entertainment, and the outcome is predictable—moms and dads who drift away from God with their kids right behind them. That's not wise, and there's no excuse for it.

David Platt, author of *Follow Me* and lead pastor of the Church of Brook Hills in Birmingham, is right:

It is biblically impossible to make a commitment to Christ and not make a commitment to the church. To identify your life with the person of Christ is to join your life with the people of Christ.[3]

God created every human soul with a need for worship and biblical community. Every seven days my soul longs to be in a church where I can worship God, be encouraged by other believers, and hear a message that helps me recalibrate my life. No matter how many activities you or your kids are involved in, leading your family to church every week needs to come first. If you neglect church, cracks in your family, marriage, and faith will begin to show. The fear of the Lord—not working out, making the team, or watching television—is the beginning of wisdom.

To have a wise beginning in marriage, make sure you both have a holy reverence for God as your number one priority. While you're dating, talk about how important faith, God, and church are to each other. If there's some uncertainty, go to a good church together or read the book of Proverbs or the Gospel of John together and discuss it one chapter at a time. Ask a trusted pastor to meet with you to explore matters of faith, because having God at the center of your life and marriage is nonnegotiable. Don't hope he or she will come around after marriage, because that's rare. I've met too many people who married a guy or a gal without faith, and now their deepest heartache is that they're unable to share the most important thing in their life with their spouse. They go to church alone, pray alone, and try to follow God's Word alone. Consequently, they've formed different values and priorities and have slowly drifted apart at the deepest level.

To have a wise beginning that lays the foundation for a great future, you have to have God in common, because when you do he will guide, correct, and lovingly bring you back to each other when you're in the middle of "worse."

Deep Moral Character

Being married is the hardest thing you will ever do, and raising kids is the second hardest. Fifty percent of all first marriages don't make it. But 95 percent of those people remarry. How many of those second marriages fail? Sixty-seven percent. Why? Because most people never deal with the issues that wrecked their first marriage. What's the divorce rate for third marriages? Seventy-three percent—nearly eight out of ten fail the third time around.[4] How can something we want so badly fail so miserably?

Marriage is hard work, and that's if both parties are relatively healthy and moral. Toss in an addiction to alcohol, pornography, or gambling, and the chances for marital and family health decrease dramatically. Mix in an array of emotional and spiritual scars caused by a sexually careless past, and chances for a happy future diminish even further. Is forgiveness available for someone who repents for past sins? Of course! But forgiveness doesn't cancel out the hard work required to overcome such a past.

That's why Solomon warns his sons and pleads with them to establish a deep moral character while they're young. In Proverbs 6:20–22, you can hear the urgency in his words:

> My son, keep your father's command
>   and do not forsake your mother's teaching.
> Bind them always on your heart;
>   fasten them around your neck.
> When you walk, they will guide you;
>   when you sleep, they will watch over you;
>   when you awake, they will speak to you.

When Solomon talks about "your father's command" and "your mother's teaching," he's referring to the commands of Scripture. From Scripture, his sons will learn what a deep moral character looks like. Like a beating drum, Solomon repeats the same mantra in the very next chapter: "My son, keep my words and store up my commands within you. Keep my commands and you will live. . . . Bind them on your fingers; write them on the tablet of your heart" (Prov. 7:1–3). In other words, let God's Word be such a part of you that it seeps into your soul and drives your life.

And then the first thing Solomon warns his sons against is falling for immoral women. If he had daughters, he'd warn them against falling for immoral men. Over and over in Proverbs, he says things like, "Correction and instruction are the way of life, keeping you from your neighbor's wife" (6:23–24); "Do not go near the door of her house" (5:8); "No one who touches her will go unpunished" (6:29); "Whoever does so destroys himself" (6:32); "Many are the victims she has brought down" (7:26); "Her house is a highway to the grave, leading down to the chambers of death" (7:27); and my all-time favorite, "He followed her like an ox going to the slaughter" (7:22). Solomon is relentless as he warns his sons of the punishment and pain associated with a bad moral character.

We live in a culture that's morally upside down. What was once wrong is now celebrated, and what was once right is now often scoffed at.

It used to be that teenagers and college students dated. "*Dating* is no longer a word students use," a recent graduate from Princeton told me. "Students hook up. Typically, you hear about two or three parties happening on campus Friday or Saturday night, you have a few drinks to lower your inhibitions, you scope out the room for a willing partner, and then you go to bed. The next weekend you move on and hook up with someone different." This is normal and expected. It's also a setup for failure.

Living together before marriage is also now the norm, and you're considered a little naive and prudish if you don't. This is the natural progression from a lifestyle of hooking up.

Every few months we hold a day-long premarriage session for couples in our church who want to be married. Of the fifty or so couples present, more than half are living together and think nothing of it. When we tell them they need to find different living arrangements, they look at us like we're crazy. But we insist on it for their own good, because living together and having sex outside of marriage are immoral and dishonor God. Research also shows that co-habitation increases the risk for physical and emotional abuse, infidelity, and divorce.[5] Statistics also show that having a live-in boyfriend is the most dangerous factor for children of single moms.[6]

While at Penn State, my wife managed a newly constructed apartment building for students. Six months into the school year, all the carpet had to be replaced, several walls had to be patched, and the entire building had to be repainted. Why? The weekend keg parties that began on Thursday afternoon and lasted through Sunday night had made the building unlivable.

I love the Big Ten and college sports, and America's universities are still the best in the world, but the moral climate is degrading. Parents send their eighteen-year-old son or daughter off to college hoping they will get a great education, but many come out addicted, morally scarred, and developmentally behind. Today's college experience isn't that of yesterday, and a lot of parents are blind to it. I've seen people lose entire decades and thousands of dollars because they had to fight an addiction, fight for custody, or fight for their homes due to moral failure. Many of their problems started in college and were carried into marriage.

A lack of moral character is a big reason why so many marriages don't make it, and the university setting is where many young people get off to a bad start. And to those who think I'm out of touch, naive, and idealistic, I ask the following questions.

Whom would you rather marry, someone who had multiple sexual partners during their teens and twenties or someone who kept themselves sexually pure and relationally honest?

Would you rather marry and have children with someone who's in his twenties, is skilled at video games, and plans on easing into a career someday or someone who studied hard, got a degree, and has a solid direction in life?

Would you rather marry someone who's addicted to porn and constantly fanatisizes about virtual realities or someone whose mind has been transformed by God's Spirit? Life and marriage are hard enough without all the baggage.

When my son's law school friends threw a party and toasted David and Sara on their engagement, one of them who is intellectually brilliant but morally searching stood up and said, "We all want what you have." They saw in Dave and Sara a purity that was so attractive that they all wanted it but weren't sure they could ever have it.

Two More Suggestions

If you want a wise beginning that'll set you up for a great future, I have two more suggestions.

Become the Person You Would Want to Marry

If you're saying to yourself, "I blew it a long time ago, so there's no hope for me," that is not true. With God's help, there's hope for everyone.

Recently, a distraught fortysomething woman came up to me for prayer after a worship service. Through tears, she recounted how she made one bad decision after another and how she felt hopeless. As a pastor, I've heard this story hundreds of times. Many people have made choices that have left them broken, lost, and alone. Mostly, they feel ashamed and unworthy before God.

Here's what I always say:

> Start your new life today, right here and now. If you keep doing what you've always done, you're going to keep getting what you've always gotten. So start today. Step by step, decision by decision, start obeying God today, and over time your life will begin to change for the better.

Then I pray over them and ask God to heal them, forgive them, and lead them forward. When I'm done praying, I can visibly see the calming effect of God's mercy and forgiveness wash over them. I look them in the eyes, as I did this woman, and I assure them that God loves them and forgives them, but now they need to do their part to obey him in every area of their life.

Be Honest about the Person You're Dating

One of the most important questions you need to ask yourself about someone you're interested in is, "What is this person like as a single person?" Is he moral, godly, and kind or immoral, godless, and addicted? Marriage doesn't change a person's character; it reveals it. Marriage often brings out the best and the worst in people.

If he wasn't sexually pure as a single person, what makes you think he'll be sexually pure as a married person? If she wasn't a one-man woman before marriage, what makes you think she'll be a one-man woman after marriage? If he was addicted to alcohol before marriage, what makes you think he'll be sober after marriage? If the person you're dating is lazy, moody, angry, and ill-mannered before marriage, you can expect the same after marriage.

"But, Bob, can't people change?" Yes, they can, and they do. I've seen God change people in miraculous ways. But they need to take responsibility for their behavior, get help, and demonstrate over a period of time (at least a year) that they've truly changed. Be honest about the person you're dating, because what you see is what you get. And forever's a long time.

No matter who you are or what you've done, through God's power, you can become the kind of person others would want to marry. But you won't attract a good, godly person while you're addicted, sleeping around, living with someone outside of marriage, and generally doing what you've always done. Start a new, wise beginning. And down the road you could have your "turkey sandwich moment" too.

12

Wise Intimacy

Rejoice in the wife of your youth. . . .
May her breasts satisfy you always,
    may you ever be intoxicated with her love.

Proverbs 5:18–19

Christopher McCluskey, a Christian sex therapist (sounds like an oxymoron), writes about a couple he calls Richard and Adrienne.

After a long silence, Adrienne shifted her gaze to a corner of the room and began. "It's really hard to put it into words. I can't even believe we're sitting here talking about this. We were both raised in families that *never* talked about . . . you know, sex and all. It just wasn't done. And we have never really talked about it with each other—we just kind of 'do it.' But it's not working well and we don't know what to do."

. . . After another long pause, Adrienne continued: "Well, we've been married for eight years, and we have a pretty good marriage in most respects. We love each other, and we've been blessed with two beautiful children.

. . . It's just that . . . that when we, you know, do it or whatever, we never seem to be able to . . . I mean, I can never, you know."[1]

Proverbs 5:18–19 uses the words *rejoice*, *satisfy*, and *intoxicated* to describe the sexual relationship that God intends for marriage. But not all married couples are enjoying a mutually satisfying sex life. About 60 percent of all couples say they are frustrated or even failing in this area. And about 20 percent of marriages are sexless marriages, defined as couples who have sex less than ten times a year.[2]

The reasons people struggle with sexual intimacy are varied and complex. Maybe, as with Richard and Adrienne, sex was never talked about, so it seemed like a taboo subject and maybe even wrong or dirty. Some couples have deep emotional scars from an abuse or a sexually careless past that make intimacy in marriage difficult. Some had or still have an addiction to pornography that gets in the way; others are bothered by a specific sex act, performance anxiety, or just a plain lack of desire. Some lack an understanding of what builds intimacy and triggers sexual desire.

I'm amazed at how many men read all about their golf swing but never read a single page from a book on marriage and sex. Or how many women read hundreds of mystery or romance novels but never read a book that'll increase their knowledge of how a real marriage works. The knowledge deficit many couples bring to marriage is, by itself, a setup for frustration.

Wise intimacy is not just about sex. Having regular and mutually satisfying sex is vital to the health of a marriage, but true intimacy goes beyond a half-hour romp in the bedroom.

Intimacy is that feeling of oneness and friendship that builds over time, and it's more than sexual. It definitely *is* sexual, but intimate sex is the natural expression of a relationally rich marriage. Couples who have good sex are usually relating well on every other level.

Sexual intimacy is all about healthy relating, but you wouldn't guess it by looking at the covers of *Glamour*, *GQ*, or *Cosmopolitan* each month. Recent cover stories included, "Make Love Last with Six Little Rituals," "Seven Sex Secrets Every Girl Must Know," and "Guys Share Seventy-Five Awesome Bedroom Tricks." Seems like all it takes is learning a few tricks, techniques, or secrets. Go to Amazon.com and you'll find books like *Thirty Ways to Spice Up Your Sex Life*, *The Guide for Getting It On*, and *Making Marriage Work for Dummies*.

Advice for improving sex is the leading subject for magazines, daily talk shows, and reality television. No other subject consumes more attention, which means two things: Nothing interests us more *and* frustrates us more than the topic of sex and sexual intimacy.

I'm not a sex expert, and at fifty-six I'm still learning how to relate well to my wife and build intimacy in our marriage. I've read dozens of books (eleven of them are open in front of me right now), studied Scripture, gone to marriage conferences, and conversed with my wife, staff, and friends about it hundreds of times. I've been a student of relationships and intimacy all my life, so what I'm going to give you are the top four ways to build intimacy, especially sexual intimacy in marriage, followed by a few tips for great sex.

Focus on Relating

Sexual intimacy is a direct result of *relational* intimacy. It's all about good relating. One year I completely forgot our anniversary, and then, just days later, I forgot Laurie's birthday. Both times she had to bring it up.

Thankfully, we're at the stage of life where neither of us makes a federal case of such things, and there's enough goodwill in our marriage to let stuff like that slide on occasion. Our anniversary landed on Sunday, which was a whirlwind for me at church, and her birthday landed on a Monday after another long weekend, so she understood why it happened.

But when I asked her how she felt, she said, "In my head I go one of two ways. One is the rational way—'He's busy and has a lot on his mind; it's no big deal.' But sometimes I go the emotional way—'It's our anniversary. He remembers his tee time for golf and finds time to write nice cards to others; clearly our relationship is second to him.' I can never predict or control which way my mind will go." Bottom line—that was bad relating on my part.

Relating well comes down to the little verbal and nonverbal exchanges that occur every day—a smile, a nod, turning toward the other when you speak. Author John Gottman calls these little moves "bids."[3] "A bid can be a question, a gesture, a look, a touch—any single expression that says, 'I want to feel connected to you.'"[4] When your spouse asks, "How was your day?" you actually say, "Good, how was yours?" instead of just grunting.

Gottman says, "Husbands heading for divorce disregard their wives' bids for connection 82 percent of the time, while husbands in stable relationships disregard their wives' bids just 19 percent of the time."[5] He says that happily married couples will engage each other in small bids hundreds of times in a day.

According to Gottman, the mere physical gesture of turning toward your spouse, even in the slightest way when he or she says something to you, is like money in the intimacy bank.[6] Turning toward someone when they speak or touch says, "I'm paying attention. You matter to me. I value what you're saying." If you have a dog, you have no problem turning toward your dog, petting him lovingly, and talking nonsense to him in a high-pitched, embarrassing tone. Turn a fraction of that toward your spouse and good things will follow.

Author Jeff Feldhahn says, "Creating a sense of closeness between the two of you is more important than anything else—to a woman, it is almost a synonym for emotional security."[7] Jeff's wife, Shaunti, adds, "It's not that the little things somehow make a difference. It's that the little things *are* the difference between feeling secure and loved, or not. The big things—some big romantic dinner for example—don't do that as much. . . . They don't come close to building the same feeling of being loved that comes from when you reach for my hand in a parking lot, or leave me a silly voice mail."[8]

Women feel insecure about themselves every single day. Pete Wilson writes, "On average, women have thirteen negative body thoughts daily."[9] And it's impossible for a woman to generate feelings of intimacy toward her husband if she doesn't feel secure and loved by him. A woman's need for positive bids is a daily challenge for men. Husbands need them too, but giving and receiving bids are a woman's emotional lifeline.

Building intimacy is all about relating, and relating is all about responding. So respond to the hundreds of small gestures that occur every day. Turn toward your spouse with a look, smile, or touch that says, "You matter to me more than anything."

Build Your Character

I make relational blunders all the time. I forget important dates, use harsh tones, don't pick up on bids, and am selfish with my time. But Laurie says that what attracts her to me more than anything is my character. I have many imperfections, but what drew her to me in high school, and what still draws her to me decades later, is my integrity, faith in Christ, work ethic, and that I put my family first. Laurie says that more than anything else it's my character that generates in her feelings of love and intimacy.

Men who are dishonest, rude, loud, obnoxious, drunk, inconsiderate, immoral, sexually exploitive, foulmouthed, and lazy are a turnoff to women. Even women who exhibit some of these same traits, I believe, deep down long for a man of character.

Solomon, who wrote Proverbs, also wrote Song of Songs, and it reads like a lover's diary—it drips sexual intimacy. In the opening verse, Solomon's wife begins, "Let him kiss me with the kisses of his mouth—for your love is more delightful than wine" (Song of Songs 1:2). This isn't an obligatory, mindless peck; she's inviting him to deep, passionate kissing—to make out with her. Why does she offer such an erotic invitation to him? The next verse explains why: "Your name is like perfume poured out. No wonder the young women love you!" (Song of Songs 1:3). She loves him because of his name, his character. And it's not only her; all the women love that about him. What women find most attractive about a man is not his body or his achievements; it's his strength of character.

This might come as a shock to some men, but most women are not into your body at all. Your body, no matter how chiseled, is not what turns most women on. Jeff and Shaunti Feldhahn recall a conversation that occurred between a married couple:

> She: "There isn't one thing about your body that makes me sexually attracted to you and want to go to bed with you."
>
> He, disbelieving: "I thought I was sexy and good looking. You always told me I was!"
>
> She, calmly: "You are. But that has nothing to do with why I want to have sex with you. . . . Really. Nothing about your naked body makes me hot—that is, until *after* we're sexually involved."
>
> He, sputtering: "But . . . I how . . . ?"
>
> She, reassuring: "Babe, I like you, and I like your naked body. . . . But it's not like my body is lusting after yours."
>
> He, grasping: ". . . What about me in my black leather jacket? You always come up to me and growl. Are you saying . . . ?"
>
> She: "Nope, even you in that jacket. You look totally hot, mind you, and I do want to be with you. But I'm just telling you, physically my body does not become sexually aroused *one bit!*"[10]

It's not your strong body that leads to intimacy; it's your strength of character. That's not to say some women wouldn't have sex with men of low character and vice versa—that happens all the time. But sex is different from intimacy. Relational and sexual intimacy that last a lifetime require character.

If either party is dishonest, immoral, addicted, manipulative, selfish, verbally harsh, or insensitive, then chances for relational and sexual intimacy are diminished if not impossible. All of us have character flaws that damage intimacy. Therefore, couples need to be patient and forgiving. But they also need to grow and change, and because none of us is capable of self-diagnosing our flaws, a good counselor is worth every penny.

Build Your History

Several years ago, Laurie and I were fortunate enough to leave the Minnesota winter and spend ten days in warmer climes. We walked hand in hand along a beautiful ocean path, and just a few paces ahead of us was a young couple with three little kids. Two were toddlers, and the husband was pushing a third in a stroller. His wife was ripping into him about how he wasn't carrying his load with the kids and how he wasn't doing this or that. The setting all around was breathtaking, but neither of them could enjoy it—they were just *at* each other because of the stress of three little kids.

I am thankful we are past that stage, because when it comes to intimacy, kids are a real barrier. One young couple told their counselor they were looking forward to an upcoming vacation. The counselor said, "That's great, because vacations are wonderful for reconnecting and lovemaking." The wife replied, "Obviously you've never vacationed with three small kids. Last vacation we did it once, in the bathroom, standing up, and there was a two-year-old knocking on the door."

It's not that you can't have a close, sexually intimate marriage during the "kids stage," but it's a challenge. The most difficult time of life is when you're trying to raise a family and build a career. There's so much going on all at once and so many stresses on your life that all you can do sometimes is muddle through.

I encourage couples to get away without the kids at least once a year, even if it's for three or four days. Your relationship needs it, and the kids will survive. In addition, ask a parent, relative, or friend to watch your kids once a month so the two of you can go to dinner just to catch up. You have to fight for little breathers like this, schedule them, and don't let anything remove them from your calendar. It's hard but not impossible; you have to be insistent and intentional.

All marriages have peaks where you're relating well and intimacy is strong, and all marriages have valleys where you're just getting through life. Gary Thomas says, "So often it isn't that our marriages are good or bad—they just are."[11] Thomas also believes that true, soul companionship takes years, even decades, to achieve. When you get there, you're so glad you didn't bail somewhere along the way, because even during the bleak times you were building important history.

During our first year of marriage, there was so much stress and conflict that we fell out of love. During the kids stage and grad school, we barely scraped by. But we toughed it out and never gave up, and we're enjoying more intimacy after age fifty than we've ever had.

Intimacy takes history, and history takes time. Not all of it is good or pleasant, but it's still a part of your history. Hard times are some of the unavoidable threads that God uses to weave your lives together, and often it's the hard times that really bring you together.

My son-in-law dragged my daughter down to the island of Dominica to go to med school. They were newly married, poor, lonely, and desperate. Nothing about their two years in Dominica was fun or exotic. To get groceries, Meg had to ride a rickety old bus an hour and a half into the nearest town only to return with a splitting headache from the exhaust and a damaged spirit from being harassed by unemployed men. She never felt safe and cried almost every day for two years. But that's a part of their history, and it built a kind of resolve in them, knowing that if they could endure that experience they can endure anything. It's a part of the "us" God is making them to be.

The more history you share together, the more intimacy you'll have. Laurie and I met forty-one years ago in high school. Our history includes:

high school football games	first microwave
young love	graduation
motorcycle rides	Meg's empty room
poverty	David's empty room
Bethel Seminary	son-in-law
first church	daughter-in-law
two kids	burying our beloved dog
Penn State	many tears
first house	many laughs

To walk away from our history and give all that up for another person is nothing short of insanity. It takes time, a long time, to build intimacy and become "us" against the world.

There were points along the way when either of us could have left because marriage was too hard, too lonely, too hurtful, too exhausting, too whatever. But calling it quits was never an option for us. The day we got married, we locked the exit door and threw away the key. Laurie said there were times when she thought, "This is all I have; I'm stuck. I better do my part to make it better, because Bob is all I've got. He's my family now." We were in it for better or for worse, and now we know why God said that.

Some couples pull the plug when they're in a long, hard season that seemingly has no end, because they can't see far enough ahead. They think, "It'll never get better, I'll never be happy, we'll never get back to what we once had." That's shortsighted. It gets better not by bailing but by building your history.

Learn to Communicate

At the risk of making my family and congregation blush, when Laurie and I first got married, I wanted to have sex just about every day. Once sex was available and permissible, all it took was catching a glimpse of Laurie slipping into her nighty, seeing her undergarments lying on the floor, or accidentally brushing up against her in the kitchen. I remember once during those early years when I must have been "putting out the vibe" and she said, "Do you want sex?"

In a rather pathetic way, I said, "Of course I want sex; I *always* want sex." I almost added, "And you should *know* I want sex."

Why should she know it? I remember talking to a friend about how frustrated he was with his wife because she seldom if ever initiated sex with him. He was upset because "she should *know* I want sex." I responded, "How would she know if you don't tell her?"

He shrugged and said, "I don't know. She should just know."

Christopher and Rachel McCluskey write about how hard it is for couples to talk about sex.[12] Many times couples will fumble around trying to find the right words, but all they can come up with is slang language they heard growing up. These words make us laugh, but we use them because we don't know what else to say. Even more confusing are euphemisms such as, "You know," "that thing," "down there," "doing it."[13]

Early in marriage, sex is hard to talk about, and many men don't know how to bring it up without seeming like sex-crazed animals. One man put it bluntly: "The male ego is the most fragile thing on the planet."[14] That's especially true when it comes to expressing his desire for sex and his ability to make it a mutually satisfying experience.

Part of the solution is for men to just get over it. Men are by nature more active when it comes to sex; women by nature are more receptive. So men need to be comfortable in their role as initiators and not take it personally if women don't initiate.

But remember that *sexual* intimacy is a direct result of *relational* intimacy. It's all about good relating. And good relating is directly tied to how we communicate. Gottman says, "People constantly send each other signals that communicate something. . . . You can't *not* communicate."[15] When it comes to generating intimacy, there are three essential parts to communication.

Verbal Communication

When a husband says to his wife, "I love you," or "You look great today," or "I like those jeans on you," it's like pouring gas on the fire of intimacy.

When I asked Laurie about this, she said, "That's true; it lifts my whole spirit and makes me feel loved."

I said, "But do I have to *say* it? Does it have to be verbal?"

She said, "Not necessarily. A hug, touch, or kiss can communicate the same thing to me, but whenever you say it, it goes right to my spirit."

The reason why a woman needs to hear "I love you," or "You're beautiful," or "I think you're amazing" is because women live in a world of comparison. Every television show and magazine cover shows women who look younger, slimmer, fuller, or hotter than she does. And men notice. And men talk. And men compare.

But the real question is, What do you, her husband, think about her? She wonders every day if she's still pretty and attractive. And, guys, you must answer that question in the affirmative every day. One negative comment about her thighs, hair, or chest goes right to her core. Convince a woman she's not attractive to you and her ability to be intimate is virtually lost.

To be honest, at times it's hard for me to tell my wife that I love her or that she looks good. I *think* it; I just don't express it. There are two reasons for this: habit and pride. But everything I've read and know about communication confirms that words matter, and expressing your feelings to your wife can rekindle the fire in a dead, nonfeeling marriage. I also know that bad habits can be broken and that if we just choke down our pride and start practicing good communication, it'll become easier and normal.

Look what King Solomon says to his wife in Song of Songs 6:8–9: "Sixty queens there may be and eighty concubines, and virgins beyond number; but my dove, my perfect one, is unique." As king, his choices of women were limitless, but he tells his wife that none compares to her. She responds to his words using poetic language to describe her body: "Come, my love, let us go out to the fields and spend the night among the wildflowers. Let us get up early and go to the vineyards to see if the grapevines have budded, if the blossoms have opened, and if the pomegranates have bloomed. There I will give you my love" (Song of Songs 7:11–12 NLT). It doesn't get much more sensual than that, and it was triggered by his words of intimacy.

Nonverbal Communication

Nonverbal communication is as important as verbal. Holding your spouse's hand, rubbing his neck, or hugging her in the kitchen often communicates more tenderness and love than words. Whenever Laurie reaches for my hand or touches me tenderly, I feel loved by her.

Often couples get out of the habit of kissing. Sex therapists Clifford and Joyce Penner write:

> Kiss daily. Kiss softly and tenderly. Kiss passionately and warmly. We see kissing as the barometer to measure the degree of intimacy and passion between a couple. Rarely does a couple need sexual therapy who were still kissing regularly and passionately.[16]

They advise that when you kiss each other in the kitchen or before work that you actually kiss for a minimum of six seconds. Make it fun and playful. It's amazing how kissing in the kitchen can rekindle what's been lost in the bedroom.

Clear Communication

I can't overstate the importance that clear communication has for building intimacy in your marriage. In the early years, when anxiety is high and expectations aren't clear, it's so helpful to say something like, "Could we agree to have sex two times a week?" When you can have a nonemotional dialogue about how often you can expect to have sex, it lowers the risk for hurt feelings, groveling, and unclear expectations. And it especially helps women get in the right mental framework for sex to take place.

It's also amazing what a simple text can do. One time I sent a text to Laurie that said, "Can we have sex tonight?" Bingo. Communication can't get much clearer than that. Laurie didn't resent it or think it was too bold or too blunt; it actually flattered her that I was thinking about her during the day and pursuing her.

While I was writing this chapter on intimacy, Laurie and I were alone up at the lake. We were reading about ten books on sex and marriage and discussing the content. We've both read dozens of books on this topic over the years, but every time we come back to it and talk about it, we grow closer; we discover new things about relating and loving. Reading a book together is a great way to open up the communication channels in a nonthreatening, nonembarrassing way.

Wise Tips

So let me leave you with a few quick thoughts that will further open up the lines of communication and perhaps lead to greater sexual intimacy in your marriage.

- *Pursue each other.* Get away for three days and read a book on marriage together. Commit to a six-second kiss every day and go on walks.

- *Let the relationship breathe.* Every time either of us goes away for a week or so, we come back with a renewed passion for each other. Nobody can be together 24/7 without driving each other nuts.

- *Increase your knowledge.* Biologically, most women have an increased desire for sex about every ten days, but it has little to do with how her husband looks and everything to do with how he treats her *outside* the bedroom.

  An orgasm may occur for a woman during intercourse, but about two-thirds of all women require clitoral stimulation outside of intercourse to achieve climax.[17]

  Most men experience a physiological build up and desire sex about every seventy-two hours. But it's not just about showing up. To quote the Feldhahns, "Men are powerfully driven by the emotional need to feel desired by our wives. If we feel our wife truly wants us sexually, we feel confident, powerful, alive, and loved. 97 percent of men said 'Getting enough sex' wasn't, by itself, enough—they wanted to feel genuinely wanted."[18]

- *For women, sex starts in her heart.* The Feldhahns write, "Her body's ability to respond to you sexually is tied to how she feels emotionally about you at the moment."[19]

- *Advice for men—hygiene is important.* Guys need to brush their teeth, take a shower, and shave their face. Basic hygiene goes a long way. Staying as fit as you can helps.

- *Advice for women—looking the best you can is important.* Men are naturally attracted to women they see every day on television, at work, at the gym. If they come home to a wife who dresses in sweats every day, lets herself go, and doesn't make an effort, she's making a mistake. No man expects his wife to become a model. A husband just wants his wife to make an effort with what God has given her.

So there you have it. If you're not experiencing a mutually satisfying sex life, you're not alone; everyone goes through seasons of frustration. And what you see in the movies is a fantasy; stop expecting a Hollywood performance that's been scripted, rehearsed, edited, and perfected. Nobody lives that way in real life.

The good news is that intimacy can be better, but you have to talk about each other's needs, talk about what's working and not working, get away together, read a book on marriage together, and try to reconnect no matter how awkward it feels. And for some of you, you really owe it to your marriage to get some professional help. With God's help, you can rediscover the amazing gift of wise intimacy.

13

Wise Parenting

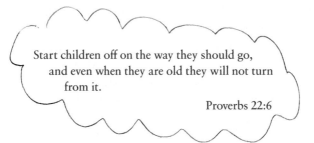

Start children off on the way they should go,
and even when they are old they will not turn
from it.

Proverbs 22:6

One day, as I plopped down into Becky's chair to get my hair cut,
she said, "I have a great story for you. A couple days ago, my
thirteen-year-old daughter, Hudson, asked if she could go to Cup
'n' Cone with some of her friends." Becky told her daughter that
it was fine as long as she was home in time for volleyball practice.

So off Hudson went, but a half hour later she accidentally pocket
dialed her mom's phone. Becky answered, but all she heard on
the other end was Hudson and her friends giggling and chatting
away. Then she heard Hudson say to her friends, "Let's go over to
LeeAnn Chin, ask for some cups to get water, and then fill them
with lemonade. I saw my brother do it once."

Becky was appalled and furious that Hudson and her friends
were about to scam LeeAnn Chin.

The girls executed the plan perfectly, but then Hudson's friend Addi got a phone call. It was Becky.

"Hello?" said Addi.

"Hello, Addi," Becky said in a direct tone. "How's your lemonade?"

Confused, Addi said, "What?"

"How's your lemonade? This is Hudson's mom. How's your lemonade?"

Still confused, Addi said, "F . . . ine."

"Give your phone to Hudson!" Becky insisted. Addi handed her phone to Hudson.

"How's your lemonade, Hudson?" said Becky.

Hudson looked around and said, "Where are you?"

"I'm in your pocket," Becky quipped.

"You're *where*?"

"I'm in your pocket—your cell phone's been on the whole time. You are *so* busted."

What Becky said next was some of the finest parenting I've ever heard. She said to her daughter, "So here's what you and your little friends are gonna do. You're gonna go back into LeeAnn Chin, ask to see the manager, and tell him that you *stole* his lemonade. Then you're gonna apologize and pay for your drinks." Becky then called the manager and told him that four teenage girls were coming in to apologize for stealing his lemonade and that he had permission to punish them. The manager was grateful, and he accepted payment for their drinks.

This mom's a hero! If every mom was like that, crime would go down, respect would go up, kids would learn right from wrong, and we wouldn't have to lock our doors at night. This mom did what many parents refuse to do: step in and correct bad behavior. After all, the goal of parenting is to raise responsible and productive adults.

Many parents say, "I just want my kids to be happy." So they give them the world, overindulge them, and shield them from any kind of discipline, correction, or work. Then they wonder why their kids are ungrateful, spoiled brats who get into trouble at school, can't hold down a job, and grow to resent their parents because they won't buy them a new car on their sixteenth birthday. A child who's given everything is grateful for nothing.

If your goal as a parent is to make your children happy, you're in for trouble. Instead of wanting them to be happy, you should want them to be responsible, honest, skilled, intelligent, moral, physically fit, relationally sound, and grounded in faith, because until they become *those* things, they won't be happy. But those things require parenting.

Becky fulfilled her role as a parent. She did what Proverbs 22:6 teaches: "Start children off on the way they should go, and even when they are old they will not turn from it." The payoff might not come until she's older, but that little training at LeeAnn Chin might protect Hudson from a more serious failure down the road.

In this chapter, I will highlight four parenting elements that, while not foolproof, will give you the best chance at raising children who are responsible, productive, and faith-filled. They're not foolproof, because nothing's foolproof when raising kids.

A mom sent me an email saying that two of her boys were doing well—they were responsible, respectful, and even got baptized a couple summers ago. But the third boy "has been on a sad and difficult journey. He's an abusive and defiant kid who has been through two treatment centers and been to a juvenile detention center way too many times. Currently, he's in a juvenile corrections facility. I don't know how much more I can take." Same parents, same upbringing, but two kids turn out fine and one kid comes out defiant and destructive.

So there are no guarantees, and parenting is hard. Kids can be demanding, selfish, and expensive, and they don't care if you've had a long day. So many parents just give up, let nature take its course, and hope for the best. But this is a colossal mistake.

Your job as a parent is to create an environment in which each child has the best chance to succeed and become a responsible adult. Every child is born with free will, so ultimately they will choose their own path, but no other factor on earth has more influence on a child's life than a parent—not television, not educators, not even peers. Those things certainly *have* influence, but nothing trumps the influence of a parent to shape a child's life and point them in the way they should go. The greatest single influence on my life and leadership was the strong home in which I grew up.

I'm not a parenting expert; Laurie and I made innumerable mistakes. There were times when we didn't know what to do with our kids; we had doors slammed in our faces and curfews broken. At times we were too soft or too harsh and thought we were the worst parents on earth. But I've analyzed this topic as much as any, and despite our failures, I learned some things. The following four elements provide the best shot at raising responsible, productive, faith-filled children.

Stay Married

I believe the best gift you can give to your kids is your marriage. If you're not married, stay with me, because single parents are some of the most courageous people on the planet, and I have some thoughts for you. But when it comes to parenting, I believe a child's best chance for success is having a two-parent family with a dad and a mom.

Today 36 percent of all children are born out of wedlock. Four out of ten children are raised in single-parent homes. That goes up to seven out of ten for black children.[1] A *New York Times* article said, "What used to be called 'illegitimacy' is now the new normal."[2] And it's what's wrong with America.

Every study, secular or religious, shows that children raised in single-parent homes are more likely to struggle in school, get in trouble with the law, be subjected to poverty, become sexually promiscuous, and engage in drug and alcohol abuse. There are exceptions but very few. Why is that?

First, divorce is hard on kids. Dr. Phil McGraw writes, "If you're a single or blended family parent, your child's life has been shaken to the core."[3] Divorce rocks a child's emotional stability like nothing else. Suddenly nothing's the same anymore, and a child's ability to feel secure is deeply damaged. This loss of security often sends kids searching for it in the wrong places with the wrong people.

Add to that the fighting and the blaming that are often associated with divorce, two residences, visitation squabbles, a drop in financial stability, the pressure to take sides, and dad's new girlfriend or mom's new boyfriend and an environment has been created that's unsettling for any child. Many kids even feel that they caused the divorce.

People say, "But children are resilient." Have you ever asked a child how they're doing with their parents' divorce? When people say kids are resilient, they're saying that kids will adjust and it won't affect them. This is nonsense.

A child whose parents go through divorce will have to overcome certain deficits that a child whose parents stayed married don't. I know people in their twenties, thirties, and forties who still feel loss associated with their parents' divorce. Some speak of an ongoing anxiety. Some are unable to trust people, sabotaging their ability to date or commit to someone. People can overcome these problems through counseling and support, but divorce is hard on kids—*all* kids. Even a struggling marriage is better than no marriage for kids.

The second reason kids don't do as well in single-parent homes is because the job of raising kids is a two-person job. If I had raised my kids alone, they wouldn't be able to add or subtract because I suck at math. Laurie spent hours tutoring our kids. They'd never be where they are today if I'd done it alone.

And if Laurie had raised them alone, neither of them would be able to skate, ski, or hit a softball. I didn't want my little girl standing at the plate in gym class while a bunch of rowdy boys made fun of her because she couldn't swing. I wanted her to rip a line drive past the pitcher's head up the middle for a base hit. I wanted her to gain respect among her peers so she'd have an advantage. So I pitched softballs to them from the time they were three. I had them throwing and catching balls and swinging bats to build their skills and confidence. That's a parent's job.

Single parents simply can't cover all the bases. Things falls through the cracks, whether it's helping their kids with homework, patching them up from a hard day, navigating their relational problems, or disciplining them. One person can't do it all.

What can you do if you're a single parent? Solicit all the help you can from your parents, grandparents, relatives, and friends. Get your children involved in activities at church where other adults can mentor them. Devote yourself to the task of raising your kids, even if that means you won't have much of a social life outside of work and church. It's a season and a sacrifice.

Most importantly, trust that God will honor you for it. And whatever you do, don't move in with someone or marry someone prematurely and end up going down a path of pain and regret. Don't model poor choices and destructive behavior to your kids. Instead, show them that you've learned from your mistakes. The only thing worse than going through divorce once is going through it twice. Get help, get healthy, live morally, and trust that God will lead you.

The remaining three elements apply to every parent whether single or married.

Train Them

Proverbs 22:6 says, "*Train* a child in the way he should go" (NIV 1984). Training isn't passive; it's active and intentional. Training involves teaching, instructing, and correcting mistakes. This is a parent's number one job.

So important is training and teaching that Solomon often starts each chapter with it:

> My son, do not forget my teaching,
>   but keep my commands in your heart,
> for they will prolong your life many years
>   and bring you peace and prosperity. (Prov. 3:1–2)

> Listen, my sons, to a father's instruction;
>   pay attention. . . .
> Do not forsake my teaching. (Prov. 4:1–2)

> My son, pay attention to my wisdom;
>   listen carefully to my wise counsel. (Prov. 5:1 NLT)

168

My son, keep my words
and store up my commands within you.
Keep my commands and you will live;
guard my teachings as the apple of your eye. (Prov. 7:1–2)

Solomon says that raising kids involves training and teaching. Some parents say, "But we don't want to impose our values and beliefs on our kids; we want them to become their own person; we want them to find their own way and form their own values." This is insane as well as negligent and a fallacy. You're impressing values on your children even if those values are "no values." What these parents are really saying is that *they're* not going to raise their kids. They're going to let someone else raise them, like their peers, professors, and reality television.

By age eleven, the average child has watched eight thousand murders and one hundred thousand acts of violence and been exposed to ten thousand sexually explicit messages on television. Kids *will* adopt a set of values. The question is whose?

Proverbs 29:15 says, "A child left undisciplined disgraces its mother." Children without ongoing parental instruction or correction become a disgrace to their parents. More specifically, children who grow up without any instruction in the area of faith and morality generally become adults without faith and morality.

In no other area do we not teach, train, and instruct. Join a sports team and you get trained relentlessly until it's second nature; join a company and you learn the company's "way" or you're gone; go to flight school and you'll be instructed until you can repeat skills in your sleep.

So what specifically should parents teach their kids? Ephesians 6:4 says, "Fathers . . . bring them [your children] up in the training and instruction of the Lord." Deuteronomy 6:7 says to repeat God's commands to your children (NLT). The word *repeat* implies that parents actually know what God's commands are, because you can't teach what you don't know.

If you're a parent, are you training your children in the way they should go? Are you training them in the ways of God? How are you accomplishing this?

Solomon says that the key to children's development is to train them in the way they should go. How's that going for you? If it's hit and miss, you could:

- Get into God's Word, because you can't teach what you don't know. Let it naturally seep out of your heart into your child's heart.
- Tuck your kids into bed each night with a prayer. Children often raise questions about life and faith in those quiet moments.
- Put a meaningful Bible verse on your dashboard or refrigerator.
- Put a Bible verse in your child's gym bag or lunch box as a source of encouragement.
- Use teachable moments when biblical values are violated on television or in music. Ask, "What do you think about the message that's being taught there?"
- Mix in some great worship music at home or in the car.
- Send a journal entry to your kids once a month with a key verse, reflection on that verse, and a written prayer.
- Lead them to church and let others instruct them.
- Memorize a Bible verse with your kids.

Why is biblical and moral training so critical for kids? Because it gives them an inner moral compass that helps them discern right from wrong. Without it, kids don't have a foundation from which they can make good choices. When your son or daughter turns thirteen or fourteen, some of their nice, little soccer friends will start partying, and your child will be faced with a choice of joining in or going home alone. Will their inner moral compass be strong enough to help them make the right choice in those moments?

I promise that every one of your kids will come to that crossroad, and since you won't be there, how will they choose? When your teenager is at a party or concert or in the backseat of someone's car and they're pressured into alcohol, drugs, or sex, the deciding factors will be whether their inner moral compass is strong enough and whether they respect you and your values as their parent.

But let's get practical. In addition to verbally teaching godly values to your kids, what are some basic training tips?

Invest Early

Studies show that most of a child's values are formed from zero to twelve. Researcher George Barna says, "By age 9 most of the moral and spiritual foundations of a child are in place."[4] That means you have a brief nine-year window to instill in your children all the beliefs, values, and habits that they'll have for the rest of their lives. It's why Proverbs 22:6 says, "Start *children* off on the way they should go."

Read to them, take them to church, talk to them about what they're seeing on television, explain your values to them while you're at home or driving to soccer practice. Surround them with other godly families who share your values. Don't hand off the parenting job to neighbors, teachers, or daycare providers or you will pay a high price later. Invest early and make the necessary sacrifices to do it.

Establish Your Nonnegotiables

Sometimes you need to sit down and ask yourself, "What are the nonnegotiable moral values in our family?" For example, where does honesty and respect fall on your list? How about profanity? What's your standard for coed sleepovers and premarital sex? How about overspending? Where does education, hard work, and fitness rank in your value system? How about faith in God and regular worship? If you don't know your nonnegotiables, you won't know what to instruct.

We had six nonnegotiables with our kids: honesty, respect, good grades, church, sex, and alcohol. If our kids were good on those fronts, I didn't care if their bedrooms were pig sties. Pick the right battles, because you only have so many bullets.

Set Clear Boundaries and Deliver the Consequences

Clearly communicate boundaries concerning the car, curfew, spending, television, the internet, and dating and what the consequences will be if the boundaries are violated. This is your job as a parent.

Boundaries without consequences are meaningless, and kids know it. Dr. Phil says, "This is your most important mission in your life. Your child must be shown with 100 percent certainty that forbidden behavior will be met with the consequences you've laid out. If you don't enforce those consequences, I can assure you that you'll sabotage your child's development."[5]

Put Home Computers in Open Spaces and Monitor Mobile Devices

Put computers in the kitchen, where they're always visible to you, and put a filter on them. Kids are getting exposed to pornography online as early as six; they see it everywhere—even on social media or otherwise innocent Google searches.[6] Many kids get addicted to porn, and it damages their entire relational future. Parents simply cannot ignore this issue. Tell them you will be checking their smartphone and internet use because you love them too much not to. This is your right and your responsibility as a parent.

Ask Questions

If you're uncomfortable with their Friday night plans, ask as many questions as you need to until you know where they're going and what they'll be doing. If your kids are still living in your house, eating your food, driving your car, and spending your money, you have the right and the responsibility to know where they're going and what they're doing. Attend their events, meet their friends, get to know their teachers, and stay involved.

Move in on Defiant and Rebellious Behavior

Parents have to constantly walk the line between love and discipline, and sometimes that line gets blurry. The best parenting usually combines both at all times. But if a child's behavior and attitude are violating your values and upsetting the peace in your home, you must move in to correct them.

My all-time favorite Dr. Phil quote is this:

> It is time that as parents we say . . . "I will not be intimidated by all the forces tugging on my children and family. I will not accept that disconnected children are just 'how it is' these days. I do not accept the epidemics of oral sex, drugs and alcohol in the middle and upper schools. I do not accept a child that appears 'deaf' when I say 'Pick up your toys and don't hit your sister in the head anymore.' I will not continue to parent out of fear that my kids won't like me if I require more from them. . . . I will not feel guilty and go into debt trying to keep them in designer clothes and toys from preschool on up! I am not charged with being their friend, I am charged with being their parent, their protector, their teacher and their leader."[7]

That kind of parenting takes a high level of courage and wisdom. But when a child is defiant and rebellious, parents must take steps to protect their home and ensure the best possible outcome for the future of their child.

Live It Yourself

Simply put, if you want your kids to be honest, *you* must be honest; if you want them to respect authority, *you* must respect authority; if you want them to be morally responsible, *you* must be morally responsible.

Proverbs 20:7 says, "The righteous lead blameless lives; blessed are their children after them." The kids are blessed because of how their parents lived. Your words matter, but you have to back them up with an authentic life.

Here are some questions you should ask yourself: What am I modeling in the areas of sexual morality, spending, and expressing anger? What do I allow myself to watch on television? How is alcohol handled, and how am I going to protect my kids from abuse? The biggest reason for irresponsible kids is irresponsible parents—parents who are dishonest, addicted, in and out of marriages, and can't control themselves.

On the positive side, do my children know that my faith is real? Do they see me pray? Is going to church automatic, or is it secondary to sporting events and going to the cabin? Do they know that physical fitness, hard work, and being humble are priorities by how I live? The apostle Paul wrote to Timothy, "Set an example for the believers in speech, in conduct, in love, in faith and in purity" (1 Tim. 4:12). How we live our lives as parents is the biggest predictor of how our kids will live their lives.

Everybody blows it from time to time. Our kids saw us fail at just about everything. They saw us spend too much money and watch too much television; they saw us fight, argue, and let a bad word slip. But Dr. Phil says, "The secret to raising a child of character is being a person of character yourself. It begins with you. Take responsibility for your own life first because for better or worse your children take on your values, beliefs, and behaviors."[8] As a boy, I never had to guess what morality was, or purity, faith, or work, because I saw them modeled in my home every day. It formed who I am today.

Stay Engaged in the Battle

There will come a time in almost every child's life when they will rail against you. Your job is to stay in the battle and dig in for the long haul. There will be times when you will have no clue what to say or do, but what you absolutely can't do is give up. Sometimes you just have to outlast them and ride out the storm.

Staying engaged is especially important with teens, because teens want all the *freedom* of an adult without the *responsibility* of an adult. They want all the freedom to drive your car, eat your food, spend your money, and stay out until dawn without any responsibility. But freedom is earned; it's not an entitlement. You give more freedom when children prove that they're responsible and restrict freedom when they're not.

What complicates this is that the last area to develop in a teenager's brain is the frontal cortex, which is the part that foresees consequences and plans ahead. David Walsh, author of *Why Do They Act That Way?*, says, "The reason teens are so impulsive is the emotional gas pedal in their brain is in high gear and the brakes are on back order."[9]

Parents have to help teenagers navigate life's minefields so that they don't develop a life-damaging habit, fail in school, bring home a baby at age fifteen, or permanently injure themselves. Teens literally do not have the mental capability to make wise decisions without their parents' help. In his book *Get Out of My Life, but First Could You Drive Me and Cheryl to the Mall?*, Anthony Wolf says, "While teens demand freedom and fight to attain it, they still need to feel their parents' strength."[10]

When our son was sixteen, he battled us about prom night; he saw no reason why he couldn't stay out all night with his friends.

"Why can't I?" he asked.

"Because you have hard classes, you have to work the next day, you're too young, and nothing good happens after 11:00 p.m."

"But why?" he said.

"We just told you why."

"That's lame. All my friends are up all night."

"Good for them. Maybe they'll learn something from you."

It was a battle, and he was mad, and we yelled at each other, and doors were slammed, and he thought we were idiots, but that's okay because he was out of his mind and it was our job to get him to adulthood with his life and morals intact.

By the way, those kinds of battles are exhausting, and many parents refuse to parent their kids because they're simply exhausted from a mismanaged, overcommitted life. They've committed to a lifestyle of destructive extracurricular activities.

For example, parents put their kids in three sports at the same time so they can stay active and healthy, but how healthy is it to be so busy that dinner's inhaled in the car, the daycare provider is ready to quit because you're always late, the housework and homework start at 8 p.m. when everyone's irritable, and parents collapse into bed without a word between them only to start it all over again at 6 a.m.? No family can function that way long term without paying a steep price.

If that's true for you, what are you going to do about it? What are you going to drop, delay, give up, or say no to in order to get your sanity back?

People have lost the art of saying no to all sorts of activities, invitations, coaches, parties, and friendships. They say yes to everything, but in doing so they're saying no to things such as rest, peace, home, and intimacy.

I hate to be the one to break it to you, but your five-foot-two teenager isn't NBA material. I've seen parents schedule their entire lives around their son's or daughter's sport because they think their kid will get a scholarship and eventually go pro. Most of these parents are delusional, and it's a formula for exhaustion.

When our kids were teenagers, we had to find the energy to stay engaged in the battle. But eight years after the prom night episode, David was twenty-four and about to graduate from law school. My wife, daughter, and I flew out to Virginia for his graduation, but Dave asked me if I'd drive his car back home to Minnesota with him, eighteen hours straight from Virginia. Honestly, I didn't have the time, and I dreaded the thought of driving that far, but I wouldn't have missed it for anything.

We loaded up the CD player with Kenny Chesney, Eric Church, and Carrie Underwood and wove our way through the Blue Ridge Mountains and eastern Kentucky, and I loved every mile of it.

After making our way past the sleepy river town of Charleston, West Virginia, it was my turn to drive. Forty miles later, I glanced over at David as he napped against the window. The sun was just peeking over the mountains, and as I looked at my son, I wondered where my little boy had gone. He was a young man, all grown up. And I was so proud and so full of love that I could barely contain my emotions. During the teen years, I thought it would never end and that neither of us would make it. But we did, and now the miles were flying by.

Isn't that what every parent wants? For our kids to grow up, graduate, and then ask us to take the trip home with them?

The battle is worth it, parents. But you have to engage. If you see your child start to drink, fail, withdraw, slam doors, yell profanities, or enter into full-blown rebellion, you can't retreat. You simply have to find a way to ramp up your involvement in their life and sit with them, talk with them, and love them through it. And you have to have enough energy to meet rebellion with resolve.

Stay married, train them, live it yourself, and when times get tough, stay engaged. Hopefully when they're twenty-four, you'll be singing along to Kenny Chesney somewhere in the backroads of Tennessee and loving every minute of it.

SUCCESSFUL
WISDOM

14

Wise Effort

Go to the ant, you sluggard;
  consider its ways and be wise!
It has no commander,
  no overseer or ruler,
yet it stores its provisions in summer
  and gathers its food at harvest.

Proverbs 6:6–8

Have you ever watched an ant? I've never seen an ant just stand around. It seems like they're always going somewhere with a purpose. Block them with your foot, and they go around it; deter them with a twig, and they go over it. When they're faced with a setback, it doesn't seem to faze them. Whenever I destroy one of their mounds with a broom, they pop right out of their hole and start reconstruction. No complaints or lengthy meetings; no whining about how unfair life is. They just pop out and get to work.

The writer of Proverbs tells us to study the ant and watch how it works. It doesn't have a supervisor. It doesn't wait for someone to tell it what to do. It just sees what needs to be done and does it. Even though an ant's body is minuscule and its brain is microscopic, we humans can learn from its example. Solomon says, "Consider its ways and be wise!" (Prov. 6:6).

Many people complain about their work and wish they didn't have to do it. While certain jobs and work environments are truly awful, the benefits to work are huge. Solomon wrote in Ecclesiastes 2:24, "A person can do nothing better than to . . . find satisfaction in their own toil. This . . . is from the hand of God." In 3:13, he says that work is a gift from God.

In Solomon's view, God did not impose work on us to make us miserable. Instead, he gave it as a gift. Think of the benefits. Work provides an income and health insurance; it builds skills, brings purpose, and connects us with people; it gives us a sense of accomplishment and self-esteem.

Most of the good that has come my way in life is due to work: the ability to write, teach, and lead; people skills, leadership skills, and conflict management skills. These have all been acquired not primarily in the classroom but by working.

Even many of my relationships have come about because of work. Had I not been working and achieving, there's no way Laurie would have married me, no way my kids would be where they are, no way I'd have the friends and colleagues I have and all the benefits associated with having good people in my life. *All* of it has come through work. Even bad jobs build something into you that you can't get any other way.

The Worst Job Ever

At the end of my senior year in high school, I needed a summer job to earn money for college. So my dad talked to a butcher friend of his, who lined me up with a meat packing outfit whose business it was to load boxes of meat onto refrigerated trucks for distribution. The job started at ten at night and ended at two in the morning, but I thought I could endure it for the pay, so I took it.

I showed up at the loading dock at 9:30 Sunday night with my little sack lunch, neatly pressed shirt, blue jeans, and tennis shoes. I met the foreman, who had Popeye-like arms and a ripped T-shirt that exposed his hairy chest. He looked me over and gave me a look that said, "You're skinny and weak and you'll never make it."

Never one to back down from a challenge, I gave him a look that said, "You're big and ugly and I'll take whatever you can dish out."

What happened during the next four hours bordered on occupational abuse, and I soon found out why this guy's arms looked like balloons. We stacked fifty- to eighty-pound boxes of meat onto dollies, *ran* them into the trucks, stacked the boxes, and then *ran* back for another load. We did that for four hours straight without stopping.

Near quitting time, I didn't think I could lift another box when the foreman pointed to a walk-in cooler where sides of beef the size of Atlanta were hanging on hooks. I watched each of the two gorillas working alongside me walk into the cooler, bear-hug a side of beef, lift it off the hook, lug it across his shoulders, and place it in the truck.

I thought, "That's physically impossible," and I hoped the foreman would exempt me, but he pointed at the cooler with a sick grin on his face. So I walked in and bear-hugged a side of beef. I somehow managed to lift it off the hook, but it was heavier than I was, and it flattened me right there on the floor. I lay on the cement floor facedown with a side of beef lying on top of me, and it was at that moment that I thought maybe I should go into the ministry.

But that wasn't the end. I left work at 2 a.m. and started for home in my dad's '68 Rambler, which had bad shocks. I flew through an intersection, bottomed out, hit a protruding manhole cover, and ripped a gaping hole in the car's oil pan. I walked a mile to a gas station phone and got my dad out of bed at three in the morning. I painted houses the rest of the summer.

But even that job was a gift, because it exposed me to hard work and made me see the importance of getting an education. During the next eight years when I wanted to quit college and grad school, all I had to do was think of that night in the meat cooler. Bad jobs teach you what you *don't* want to do the rest of your life.

I've been in my current job for twenty-three years, and while it's been the hardest, most challenging thing I've ever done, it's been a gift from God. I drive to the office every day filled with gratitude for the privilege I have to lead one of the best churches in the country with a staff of more than two hundred. There was a season about ten years ago when there was so much conflict and tension on staff and at church that I didn't know if I'd survive. I still make mistakes, and I still have days when I'm tempted to quietly walk away and never come back. But then I remember how God led me here, and I reflect on all that he's done. I know that until he releases me from it I have the responsibility to keep leading this great church with wise effort.

Since I was eight years old, I have worked—delivering papers, mowing lawns, painting houses, delivering paper products, driving a school bus. I've been a resident director for students, a youth pastor, a university professor, a seminary professor, an author, and a senior pastor. I've hired, fired, managed, and taught people. Presently, I'm honored to lead a congregation of eighteen thousand people with six campuses.

Over the years, I've learned that the most effective people are not those who just grind it out and work harder than everyone else. Hard work matters, but it takes more than hard work to be effective. You have to work hard *and* you have to work smart. There are many aspects to wise effort, but the wisest people consistently model these five qualities.

They Are Already Working

In Matthew 25, Jesus tells a story about an owner of an estate who went on a journey. Before he left town, he gave each of his three servants a sum of money to invest. He gave one servant five bags of gold, another two bags of gold, and another one bag of gold, and he told each of his servants to go to work and multiply what he'd given them.

The man with five bags put his money to work and gained five more. The one with two bags of gold gained two more. But the man who'd received one bag dug a hole in the ground, hid his master's money, and did nothing.

When the master returned from his journey, he called his servants together. When the man who'd received five bags produced five more, the master praised him for his work and gave him more responsibility. He did the same with the man who received two bags and produced two more. The master said to both of these men, "Well done! . . . You have been faithful with a few things; I will put you in charge of many things" (v. 21).

But when the servant who hid his money in the ground and did nothing with it stepped up to give an account, the master said, "You wicked, lazy servant. . . . Take the bag of gold from him and give it to the one who has ten bags" (vv. 26, 28).

We're somewhat shocked at the severity of Jesus's words and that he would take money away from the man who had the least and give it to the one who had the most. How unfair! But Jesus's message is that those who are faithful with a few things should be put in charge of many things. In other words, the best opportunities should flow toward those who've proven that they're productive.

Those who usually get the best jobs, highest pay, and opportunities to advance are those who are already working and producing. Promotions, bonuses, and travel opportunities generally don't flow toward those who are sitting at home waiting for the phone to ring. They flow toward those who are already in the game working and producing. Proverbs 14:23 says, "All hard work brings a profit, but mere talk leads only to poverty."

Financial expert Dave Ramsey says, "You cannot be the best, you cannot build wealth, you cannot do anything of significance if you don't work and work hard."[1] So if you're not working, get moving. Do something instead of nothing. Volunteer if you have to because the best jobs and opportunities come to those who are already working.

They Have a Bias for Action

The phrase "a bias for action" comes from Bill Hybels's book *Axiom*. Bill is the most productive, high-octane guy I know; he laps the field in almost every endeavor. He writes, "Personally, I've never understood inactivity. Why a person would sit when he could soar, spectate when he could play, or atrophy when he could develop is beyond me."[2]

Bill's passion is to help churches prevail. He adds, "The local church, the hope of the world will not get built by hammock-swinging, pipe-smoking, video-watching, sleepy types. It just won't."[3]

They Aren't Shiftless

Proverbs 19:15 says, "Laziness brings on deep sleep, and the shiftless go hungry." And Proverbs 18:9 says, "One who is slack in his work is brother to one who destroys." *Shiftless* and *slack* are synonyms for inaction, sedentary, and sluggish. My dad used the word *shiftless* a lot. "Don't be so shiftless," he'd say to us kids if we complained about helping out. "Your problem is shiftlessness," he'd tell us while he was under the car wrenching on something. Dad had no patience for inactivity. He wasn't a brilliant man, but his bias for action made up for it.

I popped into the office of one of my executive team members one day, peered out his window, and observed one of our youth leaders wandering around in our parking lot, shoulders slumped, talking on his cell phone. I had noticed this before. Several times a week I'd see him wandering around the parking lot, slumped over, talking on his phone for twenty minutes or more.

This was the same employee who had audited one of my preaching classes, showed up consistently late, and then proceeded to disengage in class. I thought, "If he's willing to exhibit that kind of shiftlessness in front of me, his boss, in *my* class, what's he like when I'm not around?"

I looked out my colleague's window and just blurted out, "What's that guy doing on our staff?" Three weeks later he was gone, and we never missed a beat.

He was a decent guy, gifted in teaching and speaking, but his wattage was so low that he was a downer. Nothing was happening around him or below him, so he had to go.

The guy who replaced him has a bias for action. He injected an immediate jolt of enthusiasm, built a great team, worked on his skills, read, networked, and brought his A game every week to student ministries. Attendance went from 50 to 450 in three years, and we gave him more responsibility.

They Eliminate Excuses

"The sluggard says, 'There's a lion outside! I'll be killed in the public square!'" (Prov. 22:13). The sluggard has a million excuses because he'd rather stay inside and relax on the couch. So he says things like, "I'm not qualified for any job." Then why not get qualified? Volunteer, go back to school, seek out an internship. Get moving.

Or "It's a bad economy." People still get jobs in bad economies; businesses still generate work and need good people. Become one.

Or "Most jobs don't pay enough." I made $2.00 an hour in high school at a paper warehouse, $11,000 a year in my first real job as a pastor, and $4.50 an hour maintaining an apartment complex when I was thirty-one years old with ten years' experience and a master's degree. Today I lead a large organization and decide other people's salaries. And I still pull weeds and pick up paper around the office and campuses.

Or "I'm fifty-five and too old." When most people reach fifty, they give in to the two killers inaction and excess that result in a steady decline in health. Consequently, from age fifty to eighty-five, they have poor health and then they die. There's a book out called *Younger Next Year* written by a geriatrics medical doctor. His premise is that with exercise (six times a week) and a better diet you can maintain the health of a fifty-year-old from age fifty to eighty-five. And then die.

Some of our best and brightest staff members are in their twenties and thirties, but I intend to outproduce and outsmart all of them well into my sixties just to show them that I can. And so can you. Get moving.

They Do Something Instead of Nothing

General Peter Pace of the US Marine Corps and former vice president of the Joint Chiefs of Staff led a platoon in Vietnam. Today he trains Marines to be decisive when they're pinned down and getting shot at.

He says, "One thing the Marine Corps teaches is that it's better to be doing something than nothing. If you stay where you are, you're in a position where your enemy can kill you. If you start doing something, you change the rules of the game."[4]

Pace teaches that in war or in business you can't afford to be indecisive and inactive. You can't spend another two hours mining data in the pursuit of perfect knowledge and perfect certainty. Platoon leaders and businesspeople can't afford to succumb to what psychologists have dubbed "decidophobia."

"The Marine Corps battles decidophobia with the 70 percent solution," says Jerry Useem. "If you have 70 percent of the information, have done 70 percent of the analysis, and feel 70 percent confident, then move. The logic is simple: A less than ideal action, swiftly executed, stands a chance of success, whereas no action stands no chance. The worst decision is no decision at all."[5]

You need to have meetings and gather as much data as you can, but most decisions have uncertainty built into them. Once you've done your homework, it's time to move, because wise effort requires a bias for action.

They Find Their Sweet Spot

Wise effort requires that you find your sweet spot. Golfers understand the term, as do tennis and baseball players. When an athlete connects with the sweet spot, the ball flies off the bat or racquet almost effortlessly.

What engineers give sports equipment, God gave each of us: a sweet spot, a zone, a special area. In Ephesians, Paul writes, "He has given each one of us a special gift through the generosity of Christ" (4:7 NLT). He gives every believer—not *some* of us or a *few* of us but *each* of us—a special gift or ability. When you're working out of your sweet spot, you'll say things like, "I was made for this," "I come alive when I do this," "This brings me great satisfaction." When you find a job that fits your passions and abilities, you feel like the luckiest person on earth. Talk to me about leadership or communicating, and my pulse rate jumps from sixty to one hundred. But lay out a spreadsheet in front of me, and my eyes glaze over.

It's hard to work for fifty years at something you hate. You'll be far more productive and happier if you work at something you love. What might that be for you? What are you passionate about or good at? What lights your fire?

Ephesians 2:10 says, "[You] are God's masterpiece . . . created so [you] can do the good things He planned for [you]" (NLT). The Bible says you're a masterpiece, one of a kind, created to do a specific kind of work. And when you find it, life takes on meaning. But finding your sweet spot takes time. Some of you may be too young to know what your sweet spot is, but you'll know it when you find it because it's when you feel most alive and satisfied with life and with work. So be patient and keep trying new things.

In his book *A Resilient Life*, Gordon McDonald says that it takes about forty years of getting educated, gaining experience, and trying different jobs and roles to find your sweet spot. He says, "The second half of life is the best and most productive half of life."[6] I agree.

So my advice to people in their teens, twenties, and even thirties is to pursue a direction, stay open, and try different things. But whatever you do, do something. Don't sit at home waiting for the phone to ring. If one direction doesn't fit, pursue another one. You'll be gaining life skills that'll be vital to you when you finally land in your sweet spot.

My son, David, is a lawyer in a large Minneapolis firm, and they assigned him to the trademark division. He spends ten-hour days on the twenty-fourth floor reading and writing copyright briefs for places like Target, Capital One, and Honeywell.

Clearly, Dave has a talent for law, but his heart's in ministry. He loves the local church, is passionate for the poor, and willingly shares his faith with others.

Will he be a copyright lawyer all his life? Who knows, but the exposure and life experience he's gaining as a lawyer are invaluable for ministry. He, better than most pastors, will know how the secular mind works, how business works, how people think, and how best to communicate God's truth to them. After ten to twenty years in law, he'll be one of the sharpest, most credible Christian ambassadors you'll ever meet. Wise effort means finding your sweet spot.

They Are Quiet and Steady

One day my daughter called from the island of Dominica, where her husband was in med school studying to become a surgeon.

I said, "How's Nelly?"

She said, "Oh, he's fine. He's over at school practicing his cutting."

I thought, "That's creepy," but then I thought, "How else does a surgeon learn to make incisions?"

My son-in-law was four thousand miles away from home squirreled away in some unknown lab on some tiny island making hundreds of cuts on cadavers so that someday when someone comes in for surgery he'll be able to make a perfect cut when it counts.

For three years, Nelly was off the grid. And he has got nine years to go—sitting at a computer, listening to lectures, taking practice exams, going further into debt, missing holidays at home, living in absolute obscurity as one monotonous day bleeds into the next. About twelve people even know where he is, and about four have a vague idea of what he's doing. He'll be thirty-seven by the time he's done.

But at thirty-seven he'll fulfill a dream and become a doctor. He'll be able to make a difference in people's lives. He'll make good money and be able to buy a home. He'll be able to spend the rest of his life doing what he loves to do. Quiet and steady beats loud and crazy every time.

When I think of Nelly, I think of an ant. Proverbs says that the ant has no commander, overseer, or ruler telling it what to do. It just goes about its business. It just carries one grain of sand at a time—one small step, one small page, one small lecture, one small test, one small cut at a time.

How do doctors become doctors, or lawyers become lawyers, or teachers become teachers, or machinists become machinists? One small grain at a time—quiet and steady.

"Take a lesson from the Lexus story," writes Matthew May in *The Elegant Solution*. "If you want big leaps, take small steps. If you want quantum impact, sweat the details. If you want to boil the ocean, do it one cup at a time. If you want excitement, get boring: Think method. Think metrics. Think micro."[7] In other words, practice your cutting.

Carly Fiorina, former CEO of Hewlett Packard and named "Most Powerful Woman in Business" by *Fortune* in 1998, was hired to transform Hewlett Packard back into the world leader of computers that it once was. She writes, "Business transformation is about the details—lots and lots of details. Results are about details, not big ideas. Transformation happens one product, one decision, one dollar, one person, and one day at a time."[8]

I'm always skeptical of the "latest and greatest." I'll take a staff person who's quiet and steady over loud and crazy any day, because big things get done one small grain at a time.

They Manage Their Pace

We had just concluded a fall campaign to raise $20 million for our fifth campus, the fifth campaign in twelve years. And now we were starting another one, back to back with no break.

I knew the drill and did my best to pace myself, but there's only so much a person can do. During the campaign, nobody else can write, memorize, rehearse, and deliver the four weekend sermons for me; nobody can speak at the six, three-hour-long donor dinners for me; nobody can meet with the twenty-five top donors one-on-one for me; and nobody can write the innumerable messages and thank-you cards or appear in the video shoots that come with campaigns for me.

I did my best to stay energized and cheerful, but after two solid months of writing, preparing, meeting, speaking, and enduring the roller-coaster ride of emotions associated with a major capital campaign, I was cooked. I knew I couldn't mask the damage that'd been done to my soul. I was depleted, and there wasn't a pill, counselor, or remedy that could magically fix it.

Who took the brunt of it? My wife.

She later told me that for an entire week I came home from work and all she had to do was look at me to see the anger and irritability. So for about ten days she quietly went upstairs by herself and left me alone.

A couple months later, I told our board that the pace at which we were adding campuses and doing building campaigns was damaging to my marriage and that I didn't think it was right or fair. I said there's a pace of doing things that's healthy and sustainable and one that's destructive, and we have to know the difference.

So while wise effort requires a bias for action, you can activate yourself right over a cliff. Wise effort must also entail a sustainable pace.

The signs of depletion for me are irritability, depression, insomnia, a lack of creativity, fatigue, and a general loss of joy. Nobody can function well in that condition. When those symptoms start showing up, I know I'm in trouble and need some restoration before something breaks.

In his book *Leading on Empty*, Wayne Cordeiro tells about how his frantic pace led to an emotional breakdown. "One minute I was jogging along the sidewalk, and the next minute I was sitting on the curb, sobbing uncontrollably. I couldn't stop, and I didn't have a clue what was happening to me."[9] That event landed him in front of a series of doctors and psychologists.

He was told that he had completely depleted his system, that his serotonin levels were completely exhausted.[10] The doctor said, "Serotonin is a chemical like an endorphin. It's a natural, feel-good hormone. It replenishes during times of rest and then fuels you while you're working. If, however, you continue to drive yourself without replenishing, your store of serotonin will be depleted."[11]

The doctor told Cordeiro it could take him up to six months to a year to recharge. "The only way to recover and finish strong," the doctor advised, "is to replenish your system. If you don't, prepare for a crash."[12] Cordeiro learned that there is no such thing as a quick fix. He needed to change his lifestyle, how he worked and lived.

I've had to learn to pace myself so I don't lose my passion, wreck my relationships, and collapse over the finish line. I want to work and lead with energy, inspire others, be able to laugh, and continue to produce at high levels. To keep a pace that's sustainable, I've had to do the following.

Learn to Say No

The opportunities to add new friendships, commitments, and activities are endless. But everything I say yes to requires energy and time. So I say no a lot. It's a word I use every day, several times a day. It has actually become my favorite word, because saying no allows me to say yes to rest, energy, and joy.

Leverage My Bursts of Energy

I have a burst of energy every day from about seven in the morning to one in the afternoon. I'm at my best during those six hours, so I make sure I do the most important, demanding tasks of the day during that time. For me, that's writing weekend messages. Everything else, including meetings, hallway conversations, and emails, happens in the afternoon when my energy is low. Does that make some people upset with me? All the time, but they're not me, and they don't have my life.

Avoid Early Morning and Night Meetings

I still have a monthly board meeting and other ancillary meetings that I can't avoid, but I no longer do breakfast meetings because they squander my morning burst, and I've eliminated almost all night meetings because that's when I exercise and try to get home to recover and restore for the next day. A sustainable pace requires *daily* rest.

Keep My Day Off Off-Limits

A sustainable pace also requires *weekly* rest. In Leviticus 23:31, God actually commands us to rest once a week: "You shall do no work at all." None. God created us with a need for weekly rest, and you can actually feel it. It's amazing how every seven days we all feel a need for rest.

I work Saturday through Thursday, so by Thursday afternoon my mind and body are crying out for rest. If I load up Friday with more work or obligations to friends and relatives, I am disobeying God and sabotaging my life. To be your best, you need weekly rest.

Create Margin and Learn to Enjoy It

Margin is the space between. Some people are actually uncomfortable with margin because they're so used to overlapping and running. To them, downtime seems unproductive and actually makes them feel guilty.

These are sick people.

Margin is breath and life and where music happens. Noah ben-Shea, in *Jacob the Baker*, writes, "It's the silence between the notes that makes the music."[13] Everyone needs more space, more rest, and more music to their life.

What is margin? It's a slow, twenty-mile drive to Stillwater, Minnesota, on a warm Sunday evening for no other purpose than to stand in line with your daughter and her best friend for an ice-cream cone that's piled so high it drips onto your hand.

It's sitting at home on a weekday night with your wife watching a movie because you dropped your coaching gig, book club, or cooking class.

It's planning a vacation and having enough time and money to actually take it.

Wise effort requires that you manage your pace, because there will always be more to do and you will never be caught up.

Former chief of staff Colin Powell learned this from watching one of the most beloved presidents in recent history, Ronald Reagan. Powell observed:

On Friday afternoon Reagan would get an end-of-the-week briefing from Secretary of State George Shultz. He would listen patiently but with limited attention. Around 2:15, when he heard the drone of Marine One descending onto the South Lawn, he'd perk up. It was time to leave for Camp David! He'd arrive there by 3 p.m., and short of an emergency, stay until Sunday evening. Seldom were guests invited to Camp David. The President relaxed, read books, and spent time with Mrs. Reagan. This was their time.[14]

Reagan didn't rise to his position by accident. If the number one leader in the world needed to manage his pace in order to succeed, you and I probably do too.

Be like an ant, and be wise in your effort.

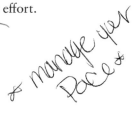

15

Wise Money

> Whoever gathers money little by little makes it grow.
>
> Proverbs 13:11

My very first job was as a paperboy. I was nine years old, and I delivered the *Joliet Herald News* to 120 houses. Every day the truck dropped off two big bundles of papers at the end of my driveway, and after school, delivering those papers was the first thing I did. I didn't watch television, play video games, text my friends, eat a bunch of snacks, go to soccer practice, or do my homework. I dropped my books on the counter, went out to the curb, grabbed the bundle of papers, carried them up to the front porch, cut the wire binder, folded them, stuffed them into my shoulder bag, and off I went. I did that every day, rain or shine, for five years straight.

Dave Ramsey writes, "Please teach your kids to work. You doom them to a life of frustration and mediocrity if they don't. . . . Child abuse is a little fat boy with his butt in front of his video games for hours eating a bag of Doritos."[1]

I'm so grateful for parents who taught me to work. Even when I didn't feel well, I knew it was my responsibility to deliver my papers. Then every other week I went around with my collection book to collect money from my customers. After a couple hours of knocking on doors, I'd come home, dump the money on my bed, and sort it.

Typically, I'd have about forty dollars, and half of it went right back to the *Joliet Herald News*. That left twenty dollars lying on my bed. Because I'd been taught that 10 percent of all I earn belongs to God, I took two dollars out of that twenty dollars and set them aside for church. That left eighteen dollars lying on my bed. My parents couldn't afford to give us five kids an allowance, so eighteen dollars was my total pay, eighteen dollars that I'd earned and was proud of.

I'd also been taught that I should save, so my parents helped me open my own savings account. I can remember checking my monthly statement and watching my money grow; it was like getting free money. So out of the eighteen dollars lying on my bed, I took ten dollars and put them in the bank.

That left about eight dollars for me to go to the candy store or buy baseball cards or fishing lures. Eight dollars for a nine-year-old kid back in the 1960s was extravagant. I was loaded.

But when I was eleven, we were at Sears one day when I saw a minibike on sale for two hundred dollars, and I wanted it. I *needed* it. But it never even entered my mind that my parents would buy it for me or that we'd finance it or borrow money from the bank. I knew I could get that minibike only after I paid the *Joliet Herald News*, after I paid God, and after I had enough money in my savings. That's exactly what I did, and that's the way I've lived my entire life.

The first car I owned was a '68 Mercury Cougar that I bought for seven hundred dollars cash when I was a senior in college. Every car we've owned since then (except for one) we paid for with cash after we had saved the money, because making interest payments on a depreciating item is unwise.

Ralph Doudera, CEO of Spectrum Financial, Inc., writes:

> Never borrow to buy a depreciating asset. People who use charge cards to purchase things and pay 12 to 20 percent interest will forever live in poverty. My longstanding rule of financial prosperity has always been "never borrow money to purchase anything that does not increase in value." If you don't have the money, don't buy it. Pray for it, save for it, and wait until God brings it into your life.[2]

As Americans, we love our cars, and if we're not careful, we'll buy more car than we need. I read recently that the average car payment is $378 a month. If you were twenty-four years old and you saved up and paid cash for a good used car and then put that $378 payment in a mutual fund every month until you were sixty-five, you'd have over $4 million in savings.

It would never enter my mind to finance a car, flat-screen television, computer, washer, dryer, or anything else except a home mortgage or school loan, because it's financially unwise.

A few years ago, I was sitting around a table with some of our staff members and I was telling them how we've always paid cash for used cars, never had credit card debt, and always given 10 percent or more back to God. I assumed they *all* lived that way, but I was wrong. One of the guys finally broke the silence and said, "You're a freak."

I said, "What do you mean?"

He said, "Nobody lives that way."

He said that to me four years ago, but now he's a freak—we're both financial freaks and loving it.

But what if you're reading these words and you're slumping in your chair because money is the number one stressor in your life?

According to financial expert David Bach, "70 percent of Americans live from paycheck to paycheck."[3] That means at the end of the month all the money's gone and there's nothing left for emergencies, repairs, saving, or giving—no reserve for a broken furnace and no cushion for a lengthy illness, job loss, or unexpected expense.

Sometimes people fall into financial problems for legitimate reasons, and there's nothing they can do but try to scrape by. But far too many people live from paycheck to paycheck because they've mismanaged their spending. These folks often look great on the outside with a big house, new car, and club memberships, but behind the scenes the debt is piling up, the marriage is crumbling, and they're one crisis away from disaster.

Proverbs 13:7 says, "One person pretends to be rich, yet has nothing." Too many people are pretending to be well off while they're slowly sinking.

How do you know if you're sinking?

- Your monthly expenses are greater than your monthly income.
- You have unpaid bills from *last* month.
- You feel physically sick when the credit card bill comes.
- You frequently argue over money.
- You constantly worry about money.
- Your financial plan is to win the lottery or inherit a windfall from a rich relative who you hope dies before you do.

If any of these statements describe you, the first thing I'd say is stop pretending and start facing the reality of your situation. The longer you live in fantasyland and refuse to face the reality of your financial problems, the harder it will be to turn things around.

But the second thing I'd say is that there's hope for everyone reading these words, because most of you have access to education, jobs, infrastructure, and support that much of the world doesn't have. If you're of sound mind and body, you can get on a path that leads to financial viability by making some wise choices.

These will not be easy choices. Nothing worthwhile is easy. But people choose to get out of debt every day; people choose to start saving every day; people choose to cut back every day; people choose to say no to easy credit and home equity loans every day.

Several years ago, I got a letter in the mail from a local bank trying to entice me into financial stupidity. It began:

Dear Robert A. Merritt [immediately I knew something was fishy because nobody calls me that],

It's summer! You've been dreaming about happy days at the lake, quiet evenings on your screened-in porch, and pleasant weather for months on end.

Now that summer's here, what are you going to do about it, Robert? It's time to stop dreaming and start living. You can make this a summer your family will always remember with a new car, lake cabin, or the vacation you've always wanted. Our bank is ready to help with the money you need to make this summer the best.

$25,000 for just $282/month

You've worked hard to build valuable equity in your home. We want you to get the most from your hard work by allowing you to borrow up to 100 percent of your home's equity so you can enjoy the things you want.

Act now! You can have the money you need in just a few days and use it to buy whatever you want. You can call us today and let us help you enjoy your summer dream.

Why do banks and finance companies send out letters and run television ads like this? Because when we take out loans to buy things we can't afford and don't need, they win and we lose. As long as your income is going toward payments on cars, appliances, televisions, boats, credit cards, and second mortgages, you hurt your ability to save for the future, be financially secure, help your kids through school, and be generous.

Proverbs 22:7 says, "The borrower is slave to the lender." The word *slave* means to be in bondage.

I talked to a young family recently who had bought a beautiful home a few years ago and had overextended themselves with debt. Unfortunately, he lost his job, and now they're so stressed that he told me, "I'd rather live in a one-room apartment than in this beautiful house if we could be free of all this debt." Have you ever bought something that you can't even enjoy because the payments are killing you?

Some of you bought too much house, truck, boat, or property, and now you're worried. Many people have too many payment plans, little or no savings, and two or three kids to educate. If that's you, what would it feel like if you knew that in eighteen to twenty-one months you could be debt-free except for your mortgage so you could start saving and be generous?

In the next few pages, I'm going to show you how to become a financial freak and love it.

Financial Freakiness

First, I must give fair warning. Getting out of debt is not easy. It takes 100 percent commitment and will probably require a lifestyle change. About 30 percent of you are doing fine because you live by a budget, save, give, and avoid debt; I'll talk to you in a minute. But to the other 70 percent, assuming you have a job, the following steps are the pathway to financial freakiness and freedom.

Get an "Oh No" Fund for Emergencies

This comes from financial consultant Dave Ramsey. "Oh no, the dryer broke. Oh no, the roof leaks. Oh no, the transmission's shot." You need to have $1,000 in your "Oh no" fund.

Proverbs 6:6–8 says, "Take a lesson from the ants, you lazy-bones. . . . Though they have no prince or governor or ruler to make them work, they labor hard all summer, gathering food for the winter" (NLT). Even ants know they need a reserve for when times are tough.

Where are you going to get $1,000 for emergencies? Maybe take on a second job, cancel cable, give up your season tickets, or sell your new SUV and get a less expensive used car.

Maybe eat out less.

According to the National Restaurant Association, Americans eat out on average four times a week,[4] which is shocking to me. A family of four who eats out four times a week at an average of $40 a meal will spend $8,320 a year eating out. That's half the price of a new car. If you cut back to once a week, you'd spend $2,080 per year for a savings of $6,240. In two months' time, you'd save close to $1,000 for your emergency fund.

The reason you need an "Oh no" fund is because emergencies happen to everyone, and if you don't have $1,000 stored up, you'll have to take on more debt to cover the expense. You simply have to have $1,000 set aside to regain control of your money.

Eliminate Your Debt

Unlike our government, you and I have to pay back our debts—every dollar. Some would have you believe that debt's a good thing, but debt is an enemy that works against you day and night. Debt is your number one financial enemy, and you need to eliminate it as fast as you can and then avoid it like it's a disease. Proverbs 22:7 says that those who borrow become slaves, and slaves aren't free. They're in chains, they're in prison, and they're stuck. To be a slave is to be in bondage.

Do you feel enslaved by your debts? Then it's time to attack. Get aggressive, go crazy, double down on it, because the sooner you get out from under credit card debt, school loans, car loans, payment plans, and your mortgage, the sooner you'll be free and can start building wealth.

How can you attack your debt? Utilize the debt snowball, which, according to Dave Ramsey and Richard Swenson, consists of a five-part process.

First, list all your debts in order from the smallest to the largest. Second, find an extra $200 every month from the same place you found your $1,000 emergency fund—sell something, cancel something, return something, use your kid's allowance. Third, be sure to pay the minimum monthly payment on each debt each month.

Fourth, take the extra $200 a month and add it to the minimum monthly payment on the first debt. Fifth, as a debt is paid off, apply the $200 plus the minimum monthly payment of that debt to the next debt. Once the snowball starts rolling, you're on your way to freedom.

Let's say you owe $9,300 in credit card debt. What if you just continue to pay the minimum monthly payments and add no new debt? It would take you years to pay everything off, and you'd have no savings and no freedom. You wouldn't be able to retire, and you'd miss out on the joy of being generous.

But if you follow the principle of the debt snowball, you can be done in twenty-one months (with the exception of your mortgage), and you can start reaching your goals of saving, giving, and enjoying. Twenty-one months from now is going to come no matter what. The question is whether you want to be in the same position you are today or you want to have the financial freedom to do the things you want.

No matter how deep in debt you are, you can get out of it, but it won't happen by ignoring the debt, hoping it'll go away, or playing the lottery. Dave Ramsey says, "The lottery is a tax on poor people and on people who can't do math. Rich people and smart people don't buy lottery tickets because they know that for every one winner there are 70 million losers."[5] Proverbs 21:5 says, "Good planning and hard work lead to prosperity, but hasty shortcuts lead to poverty" (NLT). You're more likely to get killed by lightning than to win the lottery. Eliminate your debt instead.

Start Saving

Proverbs 13:11 says, "Whoever gathers money little by little makes it grow." Little by little, bit by bit, dollar by dollar.

Laurie and I never bought anything we couldn't afford—we've practiced delayed gratification all our lives. We saved little by little all along the way, and now we're able to do some of the things we were never able to do, like update our home, travel, and save aggressively. We potentially have forty years left, but it was fifty years of little by little that'll get us through the next forty. Are you willing to save little by little for fifty years so you can make it through the following forty?

Rande Spiegelman, vice president of financial planning at the Schwab Center for Financial Research, studies baby boomers' readiness for retirement. He says, "Baby Boomers need a reality check and will not be ready for retirement."[6] He found that:

- 60% have less than $100,000 in retirement savings
- 43% have saved less than $25,000
- 36% have less than $10,000

He says there's a disconnect between what workers think is adequate savings and what they'll actually need.[7]

Not so long ago, we could rely on Social Security and company pensions, but traditional pensions are waning and there's widespread skepticism regarding the long-term viability of Social Security. What is Spiegelman's advice? Get a plan and save more. My advice is save little by little—a percentage of every paycheck—and then as aggressively as you can after you pay off your mortgage and the kids leave home. And start when you're young!

According to Ralph Doudera, "If a college graduate invested in an IRA all the money he would otherwise have spent on his first new car, when he turned age 65 he would be a millionaire, even after adjusting for inflation."[8]

Maybe you're not twenty-two anymore; neither am I. So get going. The best time to start saving is twenty years ago; the next best time is now.

Stop Comparing

Several years ago, Oprah Winfrey did a week-long television special featuring a number of people who were in financial trouble. One family had a combined annual income of $92,000 but had $115,000 in consumer debt, and this family was normative of all the others. Their debt wasn't their mortgage; it was $115,000 owed on car loans and credit cards.

The segment showed the family pretending to be well-off by holding up their season tickets, eating out at expensive restaurants, and driving new cars, but behind the scenes the cameras showed stress, fighting, and desperation due to their financial dilemma. Theirs was not an earning problem—they earned plenty. Theirs was fundamentally a spending problem. They simply spent too much.

Why do people consistently spend more than they earn? I think what drives their spending, drives them into credit card debt, and drives them into a lease they can't get out of is comparison. And social media like Facebook doesn't help. According to researcher Jeffrey Kluger, "There are more than 1.1 billion other people who mainline their good times on Facebook straight into your brain—their new car, big house, exotic vacation that you'd have to save 10 years to take."[9] When people make themselves look happier and more successful than they actually are, they make the rest of us feel like losers. If you compare yourself with 1.1 billion other people who appear to be happier, richer, and better looking than you, you'll be depressed.

Here's what I've learned about myself. Comparison kills my contentment. I'm totally happy with my house until I see your house with granite countertops. I'm content with my car until I see your new car. I'm joyful with my 4 percent raise until I hear that you got 6 percent. And then I'm jealous and mad, not because what I have is bad but because what you have is better.

The goal of advertising is to build discontentment in us and to convince us that what we have isn't good enough, and it's relentless. During a single NFL game, you are assaulted by no less than fifty car commercials designed to convince you that your ten-year-old Ford Explorer is a piece of junk. And then when you drive it out of the church parking lot next to a brand-new GMC Yukon, you *know* it's a piece of junk. Your car is perfectly fine, but almost instantly you're convinced you need a new one simply because you compared it to someone else's.

How can you avoid the comparison trap?

Compare downward, not upward. Stop comparing yourself to those who have more than you and broaden your awareness of the billions who have less than you.

Every once in a while I check the Global Rich List on Google to combat my problem of comparison. You can put in your annual income and immediately compare yourself to the rest of the world's population. In 2013, a person earning $50,000 a year was in the top 0.28 percent of the wealthiest people in the world. This person made $26.04 per hour, while the average laborer in Ghana made $0.08 per hour. Anyone who earns $50,000 a year is *insanely* wealthy compared to world standards. If you own a car, you are in the top 2 percent of the world's wealthiest people. If you own two cars, you're incredibly wealthy, and if you own two cars and a motorcycle, don't even talk to me.

Decide how much is enough. How much is enough for you? How much house, how many bathrooms, how much kitchen space, how many properties, how many memberships, how many shoes, how many toys? If you think, "Just a little more than I presently have," you'll forever be reaching, adding, accumulating, and overloading, because that kind of thinking has no end to it.

Don't get me wrong. Having nice things is great. But it was a happy, freeing day when Laurie and I decided that the house we bought twenty-three years ago is enough. The cars we drive are enough. The putter I have is enough.

Accumulating more and more things is not liberating, because the more clothes I have spilling out of my closets; the more electronics I have to upgrade, fix, and replace; the more property I have to maintain, protect, and pay for; the more boats I have to store, fix, and maintain; and the more payment plans I have to service each month, the more confined my life becomes. More isn't liberating. It's more confining.

So how much is enough? If what you have is never enough, you'll overspend, overaccumulate, and overcommit, and you'll miss the joy of being content.

Sink your roots and build your home. One of the best pieces of advice that helped us gain financial independence and contentment comes from Richard Swenson:

> Make a conscious decision to sink down roots—one house, one town, one church—for one decade. Plant a one-foot-high apple tree in your yard, and don't move until it yields a bushel.[10]

So Laurie and I did that. In fact, we planted trees and watched them grow. Some grew so big that we had to cut them down for firewood.

When you make a commitment to sink your roots and not move for a decade or more, it helps you feel connected and grounded, it keeps your eyes from wandering to bigger and better, and it builds contentment. We've been in the same house for twenty-three years, and it's not just a house anymore; it's our home.

We sometimes dream about moving to somewhere like Virginia or North Carolina where the weather doesn't try to kill you eight months out of the year. But after we dream awhile, we always say, "But this is our home, this is our church, these are our friends, and we'll probably never leave."

Start Giving

A chapter on wise money has to include a word on giving, because the Bible says that there's a God factor to financial health. It says that God honors, blesses, and protects those who give. For example, in Luke 6:38, Jesus says, "Give, and it will be given to you. A good measure, pressed down, shaken together and running over, will be poured into your lap." There is a direct correlation between how much you give and how much you get.

Proverbs 3:9–10 says, "Honor the LORD with your wealth, with the *firstfruits* of all your crops; *then* your barns will be filled to overflowing" (emphasis added). Solomon says that the first part of all we earn is to be given to God. "*Then* your barns will be filled to overflowing." There is a direct correlation between giving and blessing. God blesses those who give the firstfruits to him.

Giving the first part of your income back to God is the truest test of faith, and people who do it understand that everything they have, including their life, breath, intelligence, and ability to earn, is a gift from God. There's not one part of their life about which they can say, "I did that on my own," because they know that God gave them life and that he has the power to take it away at any moment.

Many years ago, I took our family out to eat at McDonald's. Everyone placed their order, and I paid for everything. After I inhaled my quarter pounder with cheese, I reached over and took a couple of French fries from our son, and he swatted my hand. He said, "Hands off my fries."

I didn't blame him, but I think that's how a lot of people treat God. "God, you've given me life, strength, intelligence, and the ability to earn; you've given me a wonderful family; you gave me your Son Jesus, who died on a cross to pay for my eternal freedom. But, God, when it comes to my money, hands off." And we slap the hand of the one who owns all the fries in the world and would give us all the fries we'd ever want or need if we'd just honor him first with our money.

The Bible tells us to trust God with 10 percent of all that we earn, not because God needs our money but to keep our hearts soft toward him. Jesus said, "Where your treasure is, there your heart will be also" (Matt. 6:21). God asks us to give him part of all that he's given us to keep our hearts aligned with his. Deuteronomy 14:23 says, "The purpose of tithing [tithe means a tenth] is to teach you to always put God first in your lives" (NLT).

Whenever I teach this, people always ask, "But I'm in debt. I'm in school. I've lost my job. I'm barely making it. Are you telling me I should give 10 percent?"

First, I didn't say it; God did. Second, the spirit behind biblical giving is to help us become givers, to become generous, not to meet a rigid requirement. God wants us to have a heart of generosity.

Ten percent is merely a biblical standard and a great starting point, something to shoot for. Giving 10 percent helped Laurie and me become generous so that our hands are now open instead of tightfisted. Ten percent helped us get going and become givers, and God so honored and blessed our 10 percent that we now give beyond 10 percent.

But to the person who's barely scraping by, I always say, "Maybe you can't start at 10 percent right now. Maybe you need to start at 1 percent or 2 percent or 5 percent, but commit to percentage giving so that you form a habit of giving. Start with something so you don't cut yourself off from God's blessing."

One way to visualize how this works is with an umbrella. The Bible says that if I agree to honor God with my resources, then God promises to bless, protect, and increase the resources in my life in ways that nongivers miss out on. It's like keeping yourself under the umbrella of God's blessing and protection.

Malachi 3 says that the people in Malachi's day were withholding their tithes and offerings to God and that they were under a curse because of it. But God said they could remove the curse by bringing "the whole tithe into the storehouse. . . . See if I will not throw open the floodgates of heaven and pour out so much blessing that there will not be room enough to store it" (v. 10).

I wonder how many people today feel like they're under a curse, that no matter how much they earn they can't get ahead, or their kids are in trouble, or their marriage is messed up, or things keep falling apart.

Here's what I know. From the time I started laying out my paper route money on my bed as a boy, I have set aside at least 10 percent of everything I earned for God, and I have been so blessed, so protected, and so sheltered by a loving, sovereign God that it defies reason.

And when I'm tempted to withhold from God, I catch myself and say, "Bob, for over forty years you've honored God with your money, and you are not smart enough, strong enough, or skilled enough to make it through this life without God's umbrella of protection and blessing. So, Bob, stay under the umbrella by honoring God with the first part of all he's given you."

So get an "oh no" fund, eliminate your debt, start saving, stop comparing, and start giving, and you can become a financial freak. People will look at you and say, "Nobody lives that way." But you will, and you'll love every minute of it.

Conclusion

Get Wise for Life

Trust in the LORD with all your heart
> and lean not on your own understanding;
in all your ways submit to him,
> and he will make your paths straight.

Proverbs 3:5–6

Each person is on a path that has a definite and predictable outcome. You are on a path, and that path has a destination.

When I pack my books, computer, and notes into my truck and head north to a cabin on Sunday evening, I'm on a path that hopefully will produce a book chapter. If I don't get on that path, I don't produce a chapter. If I don't produce a chapter, I don't meet my deadline. If I don't meet my deadline, the book never gets written. It all starts with climbing into my truck and getting on the path that points north. Every path has a destination. What path are you on?

Proverbs 3:5–6 is a passage I memorized as a young boy and has been a guiding force all through my life. It's actually my life passage, one I go back to over and over again. It says that if I trust in the Lord with all my heart, he will make my paths straight; he will put me on paths that lead to great outcomes. I learned a long time ago that I'm not wise enough or resourceful enough to get through life on my own, but when I trust in the Lord with all my heart, *he* will direct my paths.

There have been so many times in my life when I haven't known what to do or where to go. Actually, almost every day I'm confronted with something that has no clear direction or solution. Sometimes I need to have difficult conversations, and if I enter them on my own without God's help, I can make a mess of things. Sometimes there's tension between my wife and me; even after thirty-four years of marriage, there are times when I'm at a loss for what I should do or say. I don't know which path is the right path.

> In *all* your ways submit to him,
>   and he will make your paths straight. (Prov. 3:6,
>   emphasis added)

I need to remember to submit to him, look to him, go to him, and rely on him, not just in some things but in *all* things.

In Good Hands

My sister Kathy has the same love for the Boundary Waters area that I have and has made many trips there with her husband of thirty-six years. A few years ago, they got caught in a life-threatening storm that forced them to trust in the Lord with all their being. They were at the end of their resources, and all they had left was the promise that if they trusted in the Lord he would direct their path. I'll let Kathy tell it in her words.

Phil and I love to go to the Boundary Waters, but this year was difficult and terrifying. The forecast was for rain, but we didn't think the weather looked too bad. The Ely paper said, "Some sun, some clouds, 30 percent chance of rain."

After a restless night at an inn, we grabbed a quick breakfast, bought our leeches, and got ready for a full day of paddling and portaging. When we arrived at the access on Mudro Lake, it was raining and chilly, but we had good rain gear, and as long as the wind didn't pick up, we didn't mind the damp coolness.

We headed into Mudro at 8:30 a.m. on Thursday, July 30. Our route was to be Mudro Lake, Sand Pit Lake, Tin Can Mike Lake, Horse Lake, Horse River, Basswood Lake, Basswood Falls, and Crooked Lake. I really wanted to make it to Crooked Lake and the famous Hog Hole where Phil, my two sons, my brothers, and my dad had been many times.

It rained the entire day, and while we were paddling across Horse Lake, the rain became so heavy that we had a hard time seeing the map that would direct us to Horse River. After missing the mouth several times, we finally entered the river.

Horse River is a challenge, and the trick is spotting the Volkswagen-size boulders lying just beneath the dark water. These rocks are there waiting to snag your canoe and hold you hostage. I sat in the front, so it was my job to locate these hidden monsters and generally wake the dead with my screams of, "Rock on the right!"

We finally left Horse River, entered Basswood Lake, and set up camp an hour later. We made some coffee, had supper, and fished a bit. Then we listened to rain on the tent all night.

The morning of July 31 was beautiful. The sun was shining, and the water was calm. But the wind and rain soon returned. We tried to fish off and on, but it became futile. That night Phil made a smoky fire with wet wood, and we went to bed. Neither of us slept at all. We listened to the horrible wind and the downpour of rain that beat against our little Coleman tent; we don't know how it stayed upright. At 4:45, we got up and started packing wet gear. We knew that getting to Crooked Lake was no longer possible; it was time to turn back and go home.

We left our campsite at 6:35 and set out in the wind and rain. We prayed that we'd have the strength to get back and that God would keep us safe. We paddled hard across the wavy water in Basswood Lake and were somewhat relieved to enter the narrows of Horse

River. But we had to paddle upriver against the current this time, and the gale force wind blew straight into us. We retreated back into the river portages several times as the cold wind, blinding rain, and strong current constantly blew us sideways. This was the most terrifying time for us. There was no end to the wind and rain, and our water-soaked packs were twice as heavy, making us more vulnerable to a bad fall on the rocky trails.

There are points in the Horse River where you have to get out of the canoe and walk it up the current in waist-deep water. Phil lost his footing on the slippery boulders and fell into the river several times. I fell into a hidden crevasse and hurt my shin. Several times we feared losing hold of the canoe or perhaps tearing it on one of the rocks as we battled the wind and current for more than four hours. I wanted to cry, but we had to keep our wits.

These were hours of desperation and terror, and we prayed the entire journey. I begged God for mercy. We begged him to calm the wind. We wondered how we'd set up a tent on the edges of a river with thick forest cover and no place for a tent. I envisioned us shivering under a tarp waiting for the night to come and mercifully go.

We somehow managed to arrive at the end of Horse River, but now we faced an even worse challenge—the big, open water of Horse Lake.

Our eighteen-foot canoe was no match for the west wind that pounded onto the shores with five-foot-high whitecaps. Our only hope was to try to reach a campsite that was located up the mouth and around the bend, but the raging wind and waves beat us back into the river. We stroked and fought as hard as we could, but we finally gave in to our only option. We pulled into the thick underbrush that we guessed was a quarter mile from the campsite.

We tied our canoe to a tree and started through the thick woods in the general direction of the campsite, but our hearts sank when we approached the backside of the campsite and saw tarps and heard voices—it was already occupied.

People go to the Boundary Waters to get away from other people, so we worried about the kind of reception we'd get. But with nightfall approaching, we could do nothing except approach the blowing tarp with the people huddled underneath.

Due to the wind and the rain, the group didn't hear us as we walked into view. I said, "Hello" in a sort of apologetic tone and explained how we'd been paddling in this terrible weather and could not attempt to cross Horse Lake. We promised we wouldn't bother them and would be gone as soon as the wind settled down.

The response the men gave was nothing short of the mercy we'd been begging God for. "Come on in under the tarp and dry off," Ron said. "Do you want coffee?" I could have gotten down on my knees, crawled toward their flapping tarp, and kissed their feet.

We huddled under the tarp for the next few hours and waited in vain for the wind to let up. During those hours, we learned that these eight men were from Georgia and were lifelong friends who had been taking an annual camping trip since 1973.

As we talked, drank coffee, and settled into the forest floor, we began to feel the enveloping arms of compassion, comfort, and mercy. The terror of our journey melted away and released its strangle grip from our chests. We began to laugh out loud in the wind and wild where moments before we were enshrouded in panicked silence.

These men were not ordinary Joes on a camping trip. They were answers to a prayer that God would direct our path. They were provisions of help that we'd never forget.

It became clear that the wind and the rain weren't going to let up, so we set up our tent right next to the others.

Dinner time came, and out came the beef stroganoff, peas, carrots, and Brown Betty. Phil and I made Lipton seasoned rice. We all shared—it was wonderful. Then we fell asleep to the comforting laughter of eight good friends on a camping trip. We never slept so soundly in a tent blowing in the wind on hard, wet ground. Comfort, compassion, mercy.

We left at 6:35 a.m. It was still windy, but there were no white caps and no rain. We finished the trip all the while thinking about the eight men of mercy, eight wonderful men whom God had put in our path at just the right time.

I wouldn't argue with anyone who said that what happened to Kathy and Phil that day was a coincidence or good luck. I wouldn't argue with someone who said it was merely good fortune that at the moment of desperation when all their strength and options were gone they stumbled onto the one spot where eight men were waiting and willing to take them in. Things like that happen.

But I also know that Kathy and Phil trust in the Lord with all their hearts and that they carried in their hearts a belief that ultimately God would direct their path.

I don't know about you, but I'm not smart enough, wise enough, or strong enough to navigate life's storms alone. Even when I'm on a good path that I've carefully charted, storms come up that I can't overcome on my own.

Maybe some of you are in a storm right now—maybe something unexpected showed up in a medical exam and out of the blue a storm cloud has formed. Or there's been an unexpected job loss, financial loss, problem with a son or daughter, or a death.

Where do you go? What do you do? Where is your path leading? And in what do you put your trust when all your resources and strength are gone?

Let me show you four parts to God's promise in Proverbs 3:5–6 that can make you wise for life and get you through any storm.

Trust in the Lord with All Your Heart

Is there an area in your life in which you need to trust in God with all your heart?

Here's a clue. Usually the area in which you need to trust God the most is where you have the most fear. What in your life do you fear the most, or worry about the most, or are confused about the most, because usually that's where you need to trust God the most.

Your greatest point of fear is your greatest need for trust. It might be a person you fear. It might be the well-being of your kids—will they turn out, make the team, become responsible? If you're single, maybe you fear never getting married. Maybe it's something as simple as getting through a tough patch at work or at school.

We pray for people every week at church who are in tears over a failed relationship, an uncertain future, a lost job, an addicted teenager, or a terminal illness, and in all the fear and uncertainty, the one question that often gets lost is, Are you trusting in God with all your heart on this matter? Do you believe in the promise that if you submit this matter completely to God he will lead you down the right path? Can you, will you trust God with all your heart in this matter? Can you say, "I don't know the outcome, I don't know the future, I don't know what God has in store for me, but I'm trusting him with all my heart"?

Many of you struggle with trust because somewhere along the way someone broke your trust. They lied to you, betrayed you, hurt you, or even abused you. Some of you have been so mistreated that you vowed you'd never trust anyone or anything again. Some of you even blame God and say, "How could God allow that to happen to me? How can I trust a God who knows how I've been hurt, abused, cheated, and abandoned and did nothing about it?"

I won't pretend that I can identify with that kind of hurt, because I can't, and I won't give you some platitude like "Just trust in Jesus and everything will be fine," because it's not that simple; the healing process can be long and complex.

But I can't imagine living life without trust. I can't imagine the isolation and fear I'd experience if I couldn't trust my wife and didn't have the assurance that her heart was fully mine and my heart was fully hers. I can't imagine the heartbreak I'd feel if I couldn't trust my children, colleagues, and friends. There really are good people in the world who don't lie, cheat, or abuse others.

And I can't imagine living life without the assurance that I can trust God with every aspect of my life. I simply don't believe that the God who made me, loves me, and sent Jesus to pay for my sins would jerk me around and lead me down a bad path if I trust him. Romans 8:32 says, "He who did not spare his own Son, but gave him up for us all—how will he not also, along with him, graciously give us all things?"

As I've put my trust in God for every part of my life, I can honestly say that God has never failed—*I* have failed, *others* have failed, but *God* has never failed. So if you've been hurt and struggle with trust, take some steps of healing. See a counselor, read through the Psalms one chapter at a time, or seek out a friend or two and have them pray for you on a daily basis because a life without trust is not a wise life.

Lean Not on Your Own Understanding

Some of us balk at this because we're smart, independent, successful, and we don't need any advice. If there's a problem, eventually we'll solve it by ourselves. This "trusting in God" stuff is religious fantasy. But this verse says that our own understanding often can't be trusted.

God gave us our intellect, and we should use and develop it to its fullest, but human knowledge is limited. God reminds us in Isaiah 55:9, "As the heavens are higher than the earth, so are my ways higher than your ways and my thoughts than your thoughts." There are things God knows about our lives and circumstances that are beyond our understanding. How many times have you thought you had it pegged only to find you were dead wrong?

In his classic bestseller *The Seven Habits of Highly Effective People*, Stephen Covey talks about the danger of thinking our understanding is always right.

I remember a mini-paradigm shift I experienced one Sunday morning on a subway in New York. People were sitting quietly—some reading newspapers, some lost in thought, some resting with their eyes closed. It was a calm, peaceful scene.

Then suddenly, a man and his children entered the subway car. The children were so loud and rambunctious that instantly the whole climate changed.

The man sat down next to me and closed his eyes, apparently oblivious to the situation. The children were yelling back and forth, throwing things, even grabbing people's papers. . . . And yet, the man sitting next to me did nothing.

It was difficult not to feel irritated. . . . So, finally, with what I felt was unusual patience and restraint, I turned to him and said, "Sir, your children are really disturbing a lot of people. I wonder if you could control them a little more?"

The man lifted his gaze as if to come to a consciousness of the situation for the first time and said softly, "Oh you're right. I guess I should do something about it. We just came from the hospital where their mother died about an hour ago. I don't know what to think, and I guess they don't either."[1]

Ever do that? Ever think you had perfect understanding only to find you were wrong?

"Lean not on your own understanding." You and I have areas in our lives that are beyond our understanding. If we try to navigate those areas without God's help, we'll get it wrong and keep getting it wrong until we learn to say, "I might not know everything about this; I might need God's help on this." My own understanding is more often wrong than it is right.

In All Your Ways Submit to Him

There's that word *all* again. That's the key: "In *all* your ways submit to him." In your dating ways, your marriage ways, your career ways, your parenting ways, your recreation ways, in what you allow yourself to watch on television ways, in how you spend your time and money ways.

In all your ways, in all your decisions, in every aspect of your life, submit to God. When you submit to God, you say, "God, I'm going to do it your way. I'm going to go to church, read your Word, and hang around godly people. I'm going to follow what you say in every area of my life."

He Will Make Your Paths Straight

When you commit every aspect of your life to God—your dating, spending, friendships, marriage, kids—here's the promise: He will make your paths straight. He will make the path clear to you so that you'll know where to go and what to do in every area of your life. The longer you live like that, the more natural it will be for you to live life God's way. You'll begin to know intuitively what to do, where to go, and what to say almost every time.

I promise that God can be trusted, which is why when you acknowledge him in every part of your life, when you go to him and submit to him, he will lead you down right paths.

One Thanksgiving my daughter and son-in-law were home on a break, which is great, but they brought their basset hound, Bauer. This isn't so great, because she wets on our carpet, drives our dog crazy, and then climbs up and sleeps on my sofa chair.

I do my best to love this dog, but we've had our moments. One of those moments came on Saturday before church. I was taking our dog out back when my wife yelled from the deck, "Can Bauer come with you?"

Now, this basset hound is as cute as can be with floppy ears and short, stubby legs, and she was building some trust with me, so I said, "Go ahead, send her out."

Down the deck stairs she ran, blew right past my dog and me, ignored my whistles and yells, took off through the woods, and headed for the big swamp. I was in my tennis shoes and in no mood to chase after her because I had to get ready for church. So I yelled. She stopped momentarily, looked back at me, and then kept on going like it was a game. I ran, she ran. I stopped, she stopped. So I tried going the opposite way to see if she'd get scared and come back toward me. A couple times she let me get close but then bolted away just when I tried to grab her.

I was so furious that I stood out there in the swamp, in my tennis shoes, and started having thoughts like, "Go ahead and get lost; get what you deserve; fall in the mucky stream and drown for all I care."

But then I thought of my daughter, and I knew what I had to do. Even though this dog's a pea brain and a sinner, I knew I had to do everything I could to save her.

So I ran. I ran hard. I had one shot at saving this dog because I'm in my fifties and had only one forty-yard dash in me. I took off.

Snow was flying, my arms were flapping, and I was closing in fast. Twenty yards, ten yards—she never heard me coming. Five yards out I went airborne and dove. I grabbed her, rolled her over, picked her up, and then had a few words for her as I carried her home.

I think that's a picture of how a lot of people live their lives— off on their own, doing their own thing, and living without the benefit of God's wisdom and love. And then they wonder why life isn't working the way they thought it would, or why their life lacks meaning, or why they often end up in situations that are damaging to them.

The Bible says that God so loved the world, God so loves you and me, that he ran. He ran hard. He sent his Son Jesus to rescue us and bring us home. The only difference is that God isn't going to tackle us and force us to follow or trust him. He pursues us, but at some point we have to stop running the wrong way and let him lead us down the right path.

People who do that would tell you that the moment they trusted in God with all their hearts and stopped leaning on their own understanding and in all their ways submitted to him was the moment they became wise. They'd tell you that since that day God has infused them with wisdom, healed their relationships, and given them new purpose. They'd tell you that trusting God with all their hearts has changed their lives and relationships because they stopped running and let God love them and lead them.

"Trust in the LORD with all your heart and lean not on your own understanding; in all your ways submit to him, and he will make your paths straight"—and you will be wise.

Epilogue

If you've made it this far, I want to thank you for paying me the honor of your time. I've tried my best to share wisdom that has come through many failures and enough joy to make life worth it. Ultimately, I hope that you've experienced and felt God's love. Paul writes in Ephesians, "May you experience the love of Christ, though it is too great to understand fully" (3:19 NLT).

All my life I've been taught that God loves me, and while I know it intellectually, I've had a hard time experiencing it. But something happened during the final days of writing this book that helped me experience God's love in a tangible way, and I want to end with it so that maybe you can experience, in a small way, the same love.

For the past thirteen years, my hunting dog, Bear, loved me every single day; I never realized how much it meant to me. It might seem trivial to some, but every day for thirteen years Bear was the first one to greet me in the morning and the first one to greet me after work. She slept beside my bed and danced with joy every time I walked through the door. My wife never danced for joy, my kids never did, but every single day my dog danced for and loved me every time I walked in. It didn't matter how badly I'd messed up during the day or what kind of mood I was in. Every time I walked through our door, Bear bounded toward me, banged into the kitchen table, thumped me with her fat tail, and expressed total joy.

She was crazy about me.

And then one morning Bear lay down in one of her favorite spots next to our kitchen table, and it was over. I was hunting in Alaska, and when I heard my wife say in tears over the phone, "There's no good way to tell you this," I braced for what came next.

I don't cry very often, but I cried a lot and grieved like never before. Our vet came over and was so loving and caring toward Laurie, who was home alone. He said he'd keep Bear until I got home to bury her.

I flew home early from Alaska on a red-eye flight, and on that early Thursday morning, I opened the door from our garage to the kitchen, and for the first time in thirteen years she wasn't there. I cried again. I peered out our kitchen window, held on to the sink, and just cried.

The next day I dug a deep hole and carried her back to our woods, where we'd spent hours and hours together. I laid her in the ground, placed a couple of her sticks in beside her that she loved to fetch for me, and then spilled the dirt over her. It was terrible. My eyes are moist even as I write this four weeks later.

What I realized is that Bear's love for me was an expression of God's love for me. The way she loved and chose me every single day—undeserved, unmerited, over-the-top crazy about me—is the way God loves and chooses me every single day, and he loves and chooses you.

God gave me Bear because he knew I needed a tangible expression of his love. Maybe you do too. So my prayer for you is that you not only *know* about God's love but also *experience* it every single day.

Thanks, Beary, for loving me and giving me a tangible glimpse of God's amazing love. I'll never forget you. You're the reason I believe all dogs go to heaven.

Notes

Chapter 1: Wisdom's Wealth

1. John Ortberg, *The Me I Want to Be: Becoming God's Best Version of You* (Grand Rapids: Zondervan, 2010), 189.

Chapter 2: Wisdom for Dummies

1. Jim Collins, *How the Mighty Fall* (New York: HarperCollins, 2009), 74.
2. Wayne Cordeiro, *Leading on Empty* (Minneapolis: Bethany House, 2009), 141.

Chapter 3: A Wise Man's Weakness

1. www.rinkworks.com/said/kidlove.shtml.
2. John Ortberg, *Everybody's Normal Till You Get to Know Them* (Grand Rapids: Zondervan, 2003), 15–16.
3. Ibid., 17.
4. Bob Merritt, *When Life's Not Working* (Grand Rapids: Baker, 2011), 183.

Chapter 4: Wise Heart

1. Dallas Willard, *Renovation of the Heart* (Colorado Springs: NavPress, 2002), 13, 16, 30.
2. Ibid., 125.

Chapter 6: Wise Feet

1. Andy Stanley, *The Principle of the Path* (Nashville: Thomas Nelson, 2008), 42.

2. Ibid.

3. Ibid., 157.

4. Henry Cloud and John Townsend, *It's Not My Fault: The No-Excuse Plan for Overcoming Life's Obstacles* (Nashville: Integrity, 2007), 21.

5. Meg Jay, *The Defining Decade: Why Your Twenties Matter and How to Make the Most of Them Now* (New York: Hatchette, 2012), 5, 13.

6. Ibid., 6.

7. Ibid., 99.

8. Ibid., 10.

9. Willard F. Harley Jr., *Defending Traditional Marriage* (Grand Rapids: Revell, 2005), 173–74.

10. Cloud and Townsend, *It's Not My* Fault, 20.

Chapter 7: Wise Sex

1. Gary and Betsy Ricucci, *Love That Lasts: When Marriage Meets Grace* (Wheaton: Crossway, 2006), 159.

2. Gary Thomas, *Sacred Marriage* (Grand Rapids: Zondervan, 2000), 207.

3. CDC, "Youth Risk Behavior Surveillance," US, 2008, contracept.org/abstain.php.

Chapter 8: Wise Fools

1. Dr. Dan B. Allender and Dr. Tremper Longman III, *Bold Love* (Colorado Springs: NavPress, 1992), 257.

2. Henry Cloud, *Necessary Endings* (New York: HarperCollins, 2010), 143.

3. Ibid., 137.

4. Ibid., 144.

5. Allender and Longman, *Bold Love*, 277.

Chapter 9: Wise Friends

1. C. S. Lewis, "The Inner Ring," Memorial Lecture, King's College, University of London, 1944.

2. Ibid.

3. John Ortberg, *Everybody's Normal Till You Get to Know Them* (Grand Rapids: Zondervan, 2003), 29.

4. John Ortberg, *The Me I Want to Be: Becoming God's Best Version of You* (Grand Rapids: Zondervan, 2010), 188.

5. Tom Rath, *Vital Friends: The People You Can't Afford to Live Without* (New York: Gallup, 2005), 25.

6. Ibid., 24.

7. Ibid., 26.

8. Pastor Rick Warren's Facebook page, April 8, 2013, www.facebook.com/pastorrickwarren/posts/10151825867505903.

9. Ortberg, *The Me I Want to Be*, 193.

10. Shauna Niequist, *Bittersweet* (Grand Rapids: Zondervan, 2011), 187–88, 189.

11. Meg Jay, *The Defining Decade: Why Your Twenties Matter and How to Make the Most of Them Now* (New York: Hatchette, 2012), 81.

12. Ibid., 44.

13. Ibid., 77.

14. Bob Merritt, *When Life's Not Working* (Grand Rapids: Baker, 2011), 239.

15. Les and Leslie Parrott, *Trading Places: The Best Move You'll Ever Make in Your Marriage* (Grand Rapids: Zondervan, 2008), 46.

16. Henry Cloud, *Nine Things You Simply Must Do to Succeed in Love and Life* (Nashville: Integrity, 2004), 178.

Chapter 10: Wise Revenge

1. Dorothy Sayers, quoted in Charles Colson, *The Good Life: Seeking Purpose, Meaning, and Truth in Your Life* (Wheaton: Tyndale, 2005), 192.

2. Dan Allender and Tremper Longman III, *Bold Love* (Colorado Springs: NavPress, 1992), 197.

3. Philip Yancey, *What's So Amazing about Grace?* (Grand Rapids: Zondervan, 1997), 84.

Chapter 11: Wise Beginning

1. Maya Angelou, "Oprah Talks to Maya Angelou," *O Magazine*, December 2000, www.oprah.com/omagazine/oprah-interviews-maya-angelou.

2. Voddie Baucham, "The Permanence View of Marriage," Grace Family Baptist Church, May 3, 2009.

3. David Platt, *Follow Me* (Carol Stream, IL: Tyndale, 2013), 150.

4. Mark Banschick, "The High Failure Rate of Second and Third Marriages," *Psychology Today*, February 6, 2012, psychologytoday.com/

blog/the-intelligent-divorce/201202/the-high-failure-rate-second-and
-third-marriages.

5. Willard F. Harley Jr., *Defending Traditional Marriage* (Grand Rapids: Revell, 2005), 173.

6. Ibid.

Chapter 12: Wise Intimacy

1. Christopher and Rachel McCluskey, *When Two Become One* (Grand Rapids: Revell, 2004), 34–35.

2. Kathleen Deveny, "No Sex Please, We're Married: Are Stress, Kids, and Work Killing Romance?," *Newsweek*, June, 30, 2003.

3. John M. Gottman and Joan DeClaire, *The Relationship Cure: A Five-Step Guide to Strengthening Your Marriage, Family, and Friendships* (New York: Three Rivers Press, 2010), 4.

4. Ibid.

5. Ibid.

6. Ibid., 42.

7. Shaunti Feldhahn and Jeff Feldhahn, *For Men Only* (Colorado Springs: Multnomah, 2006), 81.

8. Ibid., 82–83.

9. Pete Wilson, *Empty Promises* (Nashville: Thomas Nelson, 2012), 126.

10. Feldhahn and Feldhahn, *For Men Only*, 134–35.

11. Gary Thomas, *Sacred Marriage* (Grand Rapids: Zondervan, 2000), 106.

12. McCluskey and McCluskey, *When Two Become One*, 40.

13. Ibid.

14. Feldhahn and Feldhahn, *For Men Only*, 37.

15. Gottman and DeClaire, *The Relationship Cure*, 170.

16. Clifford and Joyce Penner, *Men and Sex* (Nashville: Thomas Nelson, 1997), 21.

17. McCluskey and McCluskey, *When Two Become One*, 81.

18. Feldhahn and Feldhahn, *For Men Only*, 123.

19. Ibid., 142.

Chapter 13: Wise Parenting

1. Steven Nelson, "Census Bureau Links Poverty with Out-of-Wedlock Births," *US News*, May 6, 2013, www.usnews.com/news/newsgram/articles/2013/05/06/census-bureau-links-poverty-with-out-of-wedlock-births.

2. Jason DeParle and Sabrina Tavernise, "For Women Under 30, Most Births Occur Outside Marriage," *New York Times*, February 17, 2012, www.nytimes.com/2012/02/18/us/for-women-under-30-most-births-occur -outside-marriage.html.

3. Phil McGraw, *Family First* (New York: Free Press, 2005), 16.

4. George Barna, *Transforming Children into Spiritual Champions: Why Children Should Be Your Church's #1 Priority* (Ventura, CA: Regal, 2003), 47.

5. McGraw, *Family First*, 239.

6. Amy O'Leary, "So How Do We Talk about This? When Children See Internet Pornography," *New York Times*, May 9, 2012, www.nytimes. com/2012/05/10/garden/when-children-see-internet-pornography.html.

7. McGraw, *Family First*, xiv–xv.

8. Ibid., 265.

9. David Walsh, *Why Do They Act That Way?* (New York: Free Press, 2004), 65.

10. Anthony Wolf, *Get Out of My Life, but First Could You Drive Me and Cheryl to the Mall?* (New York: Farrar, Straus & Giroux, 1991), 5.

Chapter 14: Wise Effort

1. Dave Ramsey, *More Than Enough: Proven Keys to Strengthening Your Family and Building Financial Peace* (New York: Penguin, 1999), 183.

2. Bill Hybels, *Axiom* (Grand Rapids: Zondervan, 2008), 135.

3. Ibid.

4. Peter Pace, quoted in Jerry Useem, "How I Make Decisions," *Fortune*, June 27, 2005, 108.

5. Ibid., 98.

6. Gordon McDonald, *A Resilient Life* (Nashville: Thomas Nelson, 2004), 24.

7. Matthew E. May, *The Elegant Solution: Toyota's Formula for Mastering Innovation* (New York: Free Press, 2007), 49.

8. Carly Fiorina, *Tough Choices: A Memoir* (New York: Penguin, 2006), 275–76.

9. Wayne Cordeiro, *Leading on Empty* (Minneapolis: Bethany House, 2009), 27.

10. Ibid.

11. Ibid.

12. Ibid.

13. Noah benShea, *Jacob the Baker* (New York: Villard Books, 1989), 23.

14. Colin Powell, *It Worked for Me* (New York: HarperCollins, 2012), 42.

Chapter 15: Wise Money

1. Dave Ramsey, *More Than Enough: Proven Keys to Strengthening Your Family and Building Financial Peace* (New York: Penguin, 1999), 190.

2. Ralph Doudera, *Wealth Conundrum: A Money Manager Wrestles with the Puzzle of Wealth* (Winnipeg: Signature Editions, 2006), 144.

3. David Bach, *The Automatic Millionaire Workbook: A Personalized Plan to Live and Finish Rich* (New York: Broadway, 2005), xvi.

4. "Americans Eat Out about 5 Times a Week," United Press International, September 19, 2011.

5. Dave Ramsey, *The Total Money Makeover: A Proven Plan for Financial Fitness* (Nashville: Thomas Nelson, 2003), 56.

6. Rande Spiegelman, "Baby Boomer Reality Check," Schwab.com, June 26, 2013.

7. Ibid.

8. Doudera, *Wealth Conundrum*, 143.

9. Jeffrey Kluger, "The Happiness of Pursuit," *Time*, July 8, 2013, 32.

10. Richard A. Swenson, *The Overload Syndrome: Learning to Live within Your Limits* (Colorado Springs: NavPress, 1998), 78.

Conclusion: Get Wise for Life

1. Stephen Covey, *The Seven Habits of Highly Effective People* (New York: Free Press, 1989), 30–31.

A Note for Leaders

Thank you for taking on the responsibility of leading a group. It is my hope that through this study you and your group will grow in wisdom and get wise.

Before you get started, I want to take a moment to give you some suggestions on how to use this study.

Start by reading the verse provided. You can all read this together, but most likely you, as the leader, will read it. This verse generally encapsulates the teaching of the chapter and will give you a sense of the book of Proverbs.

After this, move on to the react section. Don't feel like you have to answer every question. Some might be better for your group than others. Try to get everyone involved in the discussion. Some of the questions are personal in nature. These questions can be an opportunity for group members to be vulnerable and really connect with one another. However, some group members may not be ready for this. Allow people to take a pass on questions if they are difficult to answer. Encourage them to pray about or wrestle with these questions on their own throughout the week.

The final section is respond. The books that have the greatest impact in our lives are the ones we put into practice. In this section, the goal is to get each group member to walk out the door with a way to respond to what they've just talked about. As the group leader, follow up the next week to see how they did. The respond section is where the rubber meets the road and where participants will benefit the most from this study.

Discussion Questions

Chapter 1

Read: Proverbs 3:16

React

1. Think about your life and how you use your time. Do you place a high value on wisdom? Give some examples.

2. What are the most critical decisions in your life that will form the quality of your life?

3. Are proverbs hard-and-fast promises, or are they general principles for how life works? Why is this an important distinction?

4. For Solomon, wisdom led to riches, honor, peace, health, and a good reputation. Can you think of anything else that wisdom leads to?

5. If God came to you in a dream and said, "I'll give you whatever you ask for," what would your response be?

Respond: How can you go after wisdom this week?

Chapter 2

Read: Proverbs 1:7

React

1. What have been the game-changing decisions in your life?

2. How does a person get wisdom?

3. When was the last time you asked God for wisdom concerning an important decision?

4. Who influences you the most? Do the people you're closest to enhance your wisdom or detract from it?

5. How often do you read? What books have helped you gain the greatest amount of godly wisdom?

6. What past experiences could help you make wise decisions today?

Respond: Set up a meeting this week with a person who can help you gain wisdom in one area of your life. Go prepared with a list of questions and a way to take notes.

Chapter 3

Read: 1 Kings 11:3

React

1. This chapter states that "no amount of wisdom can withstand the pull that sin has when it hooks into our emotional 'want to.'" What are the most common examples of when people forfeit their long-term future for an emotional "want to" in the moment?

2. Why do extremely wise and intelligent people sometimes do such foolish things?

3. What wisdom have you gained through experience and pain?

4. Has there been a time in your life when a way that seemed right to you led to destruction (Prov. 16:25)?

5. What's a weakness in your life that if left unchecked or unmanaged could become your undoing?

Respond: Spend this week determining what your greatest weakness is. Then write down a plan that can help you confront or manage this weakness so that it doesn't lead to your undoing. You may want to find an accountability partner who can help you adhere to this plan.

Chapter 4

Read: Proverbs 4:23

React

1. Give some examples of ways to "guard your heart."

2. What are the top three things that dominate your thinking?

3. How could you begin to take every thought captive?

4. What are some areas of your life in which you control your feelings, and what are some areas in which your feelings are prone to control you?

5. How's your heart these days? Provide one or two words or emotions that would describe your heart.

Respond: Overload your mind with images, thoughts, and experiences (worship experiences, verses, biblical teaching, and conversations with Christian friends) that are holy and pure.

Write out five indicators of heart health. What are the signs that your heart is pure and godly, and what are the signs that your heart is drifting away from God?

Chapter 5

Read: Proverbs 12:18

React

1. In general, have you done more damage in life by what you've said or what you've done?

2. When or where are you the most prone to use hurtful or reckless words?

3. What are the benefits of watching your words?

4. How do you see your words affecting people closest to you?

5. How kind, gentle, and encouraging are your words these days (with your spouse, kids, co-workers, and friends)?

Respond: Think of one person who could use your encouragement this week, and then do it!

Chapter 6

Read: Proverbs 4:26

React

1. What are your well-worn paths? List your top three.

2. What are the main influences (people, places, or habits) that keep you on your well-worn paths?

3. Are you on a path right now that you need to stop traveling? What decision do you need to make today to get off of that path?

4. Are you currently being tempted to swerve off a good path? What do you need to do to stay on track?

Respond: If you're in your twenties, write down the one path you need to get on, or off, to get to where you want to be in your thirties or forties. If you're beyond your twenties, same question.

Chapter 7

Read: Proverbs 5:18–19

React

1. How does the Bible define "wise sex"?

2. What are the benefits of sexual purity? What are the consequences of sexual impurity?

3. What happens when you shut off all other sexual images and focus exclusively on your spouse?

Respond: Find a person who could hold you accountable in your pursuit of sexual purity.

Chapter 8

Read: Proverbs 17:12

React

1. What's the difference between being a fool and being foolish?

2. What are the characteristics of a fool?

3. Is there a fool in your life right now? How should you deal with that person?

4. Of all the characteristics of a fool described in this chapter, which one most frequently surfaces in your life?

5. Are you a fool? How would you know?

6. What repeat patterns in your life have hurt your relationships and impeded your progress? In other words, what's the one thing that gets you in trouble more than anything else?

Respond: Apologize to someone and repent of a sin that has hurt other people in your life.

Chapter 9

Read: Proverbs 17:17

React

1. Describe a time when you felt alone.

2. Who are your closest friends? Who are your 2 a.m. friends?

3. Do you have a few close friends or lots of acquaintances?

4. In this chapter, Bob lists three common forms of loneliness—situational, seasonal, and chronic. Of these three, which one has been the most prevalent in your life over the last ten years? Describe what that felt like.

5. Who are the friends in your life who sharpen and challenge you to get better?

6. What's one thing about you that hurts your friendships?

Respond: Take the friendship inventory on page 114. If you can't say yes to most of the questions, join a small group or take a relational risk this week and ask someone to coffee.

Chapter 10

Read: Proverbs 20:22

React

1. What's the difference between a righteous sort of anger and a sinful one?

2. What's the ultimate goal of "wise revenge"?

3. Would you say that you regularly place a higher value on relationships or on revenge? Give an example.

4. Is there anyone in your life right now toward whom you feel strong negative feelings? What would be the best approach in dealing with that person?

5. Who are the critics in your life? What's a godly response to criticism?

Respond: Name one person in your life who's been critical of you. Respond to them this week in the manner outlined in this chapter.

Chapter 11

Read: Proverbs 6:20

React

1. If you're single, how could you become more like the person you'd want to marry? If you're married, what would it take for you to become the right person for your spouse and family?

2. What's the most important ingredient in a happy marriage?

3. How would you describe your commitment to a local church? All in? Sporadic?

4. What would it look like for Christ to be at the center of your relationship? Is it that way right now?

5. Describe (in as much detail as possible) the vision you have for your marriage. (You can do this if you're single or married.) What needs to change for that vision to become a reality?

Respond: If you're single, write out a list of the characteristics you're looking for in a future spouse. Then pick one of them to work on in your own life.

If you're married, go on a date with your spouse this week. Talk about the content of this chapter. Specifically, talk about the ingredients you need in order to have a great marriage.

Chapter 12

Read: Proverbs 5:18–19

React

1. How comfortable are you talking about sex? Was sex talked about in a healthy way in your home growing up?

2. On a scale of 1 to 10, how would you rank the relational intimacy in your marriage? What's one thing you could do to improve it?

3. In what ways is your character enhancing or diminishing the relational/sexual intimacy in your marriage?

4. Have you ever been tempted to walk away from your relationship? Take a moment to write out your history together.

5. What would it look like to pursue your spouse this week?

Respond: Get a babysitter, if needed, and go out to dinner with your spouse this week. Discuss the contents of this chapter and talk about what you need/want in the areas of sexual and relational intimacy.

Chapter 13

Read: Proverbs 22:6

React

1. What's the goal of parenting? What's *not* the goal?

2. What are some of the bad behaviors in your children that you've let slide? How could you start stepping in to correct them this week?

3. What are the nonnegotiable moral values in your family?

4. What are you modeling for your children in the areas of sexual morality, spending, anger, television, alcohol, church, and faith?

5. Is your family exhausted from all the extracurricular activities? What do you need to drop, delay, give up, or say no to?

Respond: Read Bob's suggestions on page 170 for training your child in the Lord. Pick one and start implementing it this week.

Chapter 14

Read: Proverbs 22:7

React

1. What are the benefits of work?

2. Do you have a bias for action, and what does that look like in your life?

3. What would you say is the most frequent excuse you make that prevents you from being more productive?

4. Describe your sweet spot.

5. Is the pace at which you're working healthy and sustainable? If not, what steps could you take to get to a healthy place?

6. What are some signs of depletion for you? Are you experiencing any right now?

Respond: Look over your calendar from the past month. How well did you manage your pace and energy? What needs to be cut from your schedule? What needs to be added? And what needs to be moved to a different time in order to maximize your energy bursts?

Chapter 15

Read: Proverbs 13:11

React

1. Do you live from paycheck to paycheck, or do you have financial margin?

2. What's your view of debt? What's God's view?

3. In what area of your life do you need to practice delayed gratification?

4. Is your attitude toward God "hands off" when it comes to money, or are you a giver?

5. Do you believe that God deserves and will bless those who set aside 10 percent of their income for him?

Respond: Ask yourself, "How much is enough for me?" Write down all the areas of your life (house, car, etc.) where what you have right now is enough. Then when your income increases, commit to raising your standard of giving instead of your standard of living.

Conclusion

Read: Proverbs 3:5–6

React

1. What paths are you on right now? If you keep going in the direction you are going, what are the predictable outcomes (in your career, marriage, relationship with your kids, relationships with friends, etc.)?

2. What do you fear the most? What would it look like to trust God in this area of your life?

3. Is there an area of your life in which you have withheld your trust and kept God at a distance because of past hurts? What would it take to receive healing in this area?

4. Do you submit to God in all your ways or just in some?

5. Can you think of a time when God failed you? If not, why would he ever fail you in the future?

Respond: Have you ever had a moment in your life when you acknowledged to God that you were running the wrong way, leaning on your own understanding, and not trusting Christ with your whole heart? If not, pray this prayer. "Lord Jesus, I have been running the wrong way. I have been leaning on my own understanding and not yours. But in this moment, I want to turn from all that. I trust you, Christ, with my whole heart. I believe that you died on the cross to pay the penalty for sin that I deserved. In this moment, I receive the forgiveness and eternal life that you offer. Amen."

Bob Merritt has been the senior pastor of Eagle Brook Church, outside St. Paul, MN, since 1991, leading the church through a period of explosive growth. In his messages, he tackles tough topics and answers life-changing questions about faith, family, and much more—while keeping the church's mission to reach others for Christ at the forefront. He holds an MA in divinity from Bethel Seminary and a PhD in speech communications from Pennsylvania State University. Bob and his wife, Laurie, live in White Bear Lake and have two adult children. Bob does not tweet.

Visit Bob Merritt at bobmerritt.net.

Also By
BOB MERRITT

In this positive, insightful book, pastor Bob Merritt describes seven foundational choices that will set you up for the best possible outcomes in work, school, relationships, and life.